F.I.E.R.C.E
MOTHERS

Create the Life of Your Dreams and
Crush Your Goals

Ugochi Onyewu

Scripture quotations are from *The Holy Bible, New International Version* ®, Copyright © 1973, 1978, 1984 by International Bible Society

ISBN: 978-1-7342285-0-2

Dedication

I want to give a special thanks to the following people who have made the biggest difference in my life.

Emeka—*My original "Ride or Die" life partner. No exchange, no refund. What a ride, babe. I love you.*

My children, Ezra, Azure, and Noah—*You are my support system and without you, nothing makes any sense. You inspire me each day to keep going and give me a reason for it all. I love you guys.*

Mummy—*Thank you for everything. You have always been there for us, and now that I am a Mother, I can appreciate all the sacrifices you made. Lots of love.*

My sister Yoyo, Destiny, Chika, Bunmi, Ada and my bible study sisters—*Having you ladies in my life makes all the difference.*

My "Day Ones"—*My girls who jumped at the chance to support me when there was nothing in it for them. You agreed to take part because I asked you to. My "First Ten," I call them: Yoyo, Chika, Destiny, RiRi,*

Adanna, Chi-Chi, Chioma, Kwavi, Ada Ibe, and Ada. I love you ladies, and I will always be grateful.

Ngozi—*Thanks for the fantastic idea to share my experiences.*

DOWNLOAD THE AUDIOBOOK FOR FREE!

Just to say *thank you* for buying my book, I would like to give you the audiobook version 100% FREE!

To **download this free audiobook** go to:
http://fiercemothers.com/audiobook

Contents

Huge Favor!... 241

Introduction

Are you a Mother trying to achieve your life goals but finding that you are overwhelmed and exhausted from taking care of your family? Do you feel like your life has been put on hold? You may even feel like this, where you currently are, is just it for you. You need to learn a new approach to life that enables you to achieve your goals and still be a rock star Mother. This really changes everything. Believe me from the bottom of my heart when I say you **will** get your life back.

I see you. I am not there right now with you at this moment, but I can relate to your struggles.

In this book, I will teach you how to pursue your dreams without burning out. We will go on a journey together to discover how you can achieve that. It is possible to bring your dreams to fruition without feeling overwhelmed or experiencing burnout.

Mindset is the key to achieving the life of your dreams. And that life **is** attainable. It is much easier to achieve your dreams when you have someone like me to walk you through the process. I've been through it myself. I've experienced the challenges of striving for goals that don't seem attainable. I've faced those challenges with young children and now with older children. Doing this in addition to the demands of everyday life can leave you exhausted and make you feel stuck. But I have experienced this journey, and now I'm providing you the tools that I have used to make that journey successful.

I often wish that I had discovered a book like this in the earlier years of Motherhood. There were times that I felt so alone and so discouraged. Then, I believed that no one could understand how I felt. Often I felt that there was no one to talk to. I wrote this book from that position—know you are not alone.

Here is what I would say to you now.

- **Apply for that job. Go back to school. Start that hobby.** Write that book or memoir. Put yourself out there. Do it now when it is the absolute toughest time to do it. You have so many things on your plate already, and you are trying to get through each day. There will never be a good time to work toward your goals. Start small, but start. Allow yourself to strive for that goal that always seems to be on the back burner. The goal is achievable and waiting for you, but you have to begin somewhere.

- **Fail often, fail fast.** Give yourself permission to go for your goals even if you think you might fail. When you fail, pick yourself up and keep going. My sister shared important advice with me—she has learned that it does not have to be an all-or-nothing approach to achieving goals. I agree with her. You can perform a task that moves you forward for as little as ten minutes a day. In that short time, it will create the spark that you need to keep going.

- **Try new things.** I also say that you should be daring and do the things that embarrass you. The more you do these things, the more it will take away the fear of other people's opinions. Achieving the goals that you dream about takes time. It truly is a journey. Part of the delay in setting out to accomplish your goals could be the fear of judgement, or worrying about what other people may think about what you create. It certainly was an issue for me. It was hard, but I learned to care less about how other people view me. Trust me—everyone is too busy worrying about how other people view them, and they don't care about you and your journey.

- **Envision a new reality.** Imagine what it would feel like to achieve the goals that you find yourself dreaming about. You will have a renewed sense of purpose and confidence. You will face life knowing that in spite of the challenges, you have accomplished what you set out to do. You will make new goals knowing that you are able to work hard and achieve anything. After all, you already know you can accomplish things. Life becomes an adventure instead of a chore. You are now able to help other people and become an authority in whatever field you excel.

- **Develop new habits.** The journey to accomplishing your goals will change you as an individual. It will help you develop discipline and habits—habits that you would not have developed otherwise. In fact, the journey is more important than the destination.

You will emerge from this journey as a transformed person.

I promise you that the biggest gift I can give you is the gift of a renewed sense of purpose. You will come away from this book knowing that you are here on earth for a purpose. You will believe in a way that you never have before that your destiny awaits. You have an assignment that only you can fulfill.

In this book, I will provide specific calls to action. This will help you build a roadmap for your individual journey.

The F.I.E.R.C.E Methodology

I use the acronym **F.I.E.R.C.E** as a framework for this book. Follow the steps and exercises in each section, and you too will become a **F.I.E.R.C.E** Mother. A F.I.E.R.C.E Mother is one who stands firm in her assigned place on earth.

F for First Things First. This will make you question the reason for it all. It will replace the mindset of drudgery with a sense of purpose and intention. You'll learn how to change questions into motivating calls to action:

- How long before the children are in bed and I can sit down and watch TV? → What small step towards my goal can I accomplish?

- How long until this day is over and I can go home? → What did I do well today, and why was I successful?

- How long until Friday? →What are some of the action items on my list that I can get done before the weekend?

I for I Am. Knowing who you are will ground you and make you resistant to other people's opinions of you. It will lead to a greater ability to self-affirm. **This** will give you a clear picture of who you are and make it clear why this is important.

E for Engine. This discusses the powerhouse that you are. It will teach you the importance of maintaining your engine. You cannot give what you do not have, and it is critical to ensure that you keep your engine in prime condition.

R for Relationships. This emphasizes the importance of other people in our lives. We are not created to exist in isolation, and we cannot succeed alone. Relationships with others will also provide a source of encouragement and accountability to do what you set out to do.

C for Chief Financial Officer. This teaches you how to be a boss in the area of your finances. You are the Chief Financial Officer of your life. Becoming a financial boss will lead you to the success you desire in other areas of your life.

E for Execution. This teaches you that knowledge without action is wasted. This is not a feel-good book. Instead, this book prompts you to take specific actions to achieve the next level of what is in store for you. You will go beyond feeling good and be motivated to make decisions to propel you forward on your journey.

I make a big promise to you by setting you on a journey to success. Adopt an open mind and embrace the simplicity of my message. Do the exercises, and this book will change your life.

Your journey should start now—not tomorrow, or next week, or next year, or when things calm down a little. The quicker you start, the sooner you'll get into the rhythm of what works for you. Don't wait because there will never be a good time. It will always be hard, so begin your journey. I know you can do it!

My Story

As I sit writing this, I doubt what gives me the qualifications to write this book. I question whether anyone cares what I have to say. I am writing from a place of vulnerability, but I have to get this story out. I am confident that this message is effective and will change lives.

This book will take you through the specific principles that I have applied in my own life to achieve the following:

- Run ten full marathons, fourteen half marathons, and four ten-mile races.

- Start an interview format podcast celebrating Igbo[1] culture and Igbo women.

- Complete my MBA and graduate with my class. I did this despite being pregnant with twins and delivering my twins in my first year of business school.

- Give of my time, talent, and treasure.

- Sponsor ten-year-old twins in Haiti and visit Haiti twice on a mission trip.

- Partner with a dear friend who is the founder of a charity organization in Nigeria. This organization helps orphaned children and the less fortunate.

---

[1] Igbo Culture is the traditions of the Igbo People, a tribe in South Eastern Nigeria.

- Work full time in a challenging and demanding role.

- Have very close and precious relationships with all three of my children

- Experience a joyful marriage that works (although, it's not perfect).

It has not been easy at all, and I do not want you to think that my life is glamorous. I do it "ugly." This means that a lot of the time I have no idea what I am doing. Often I will try something new and the result is an unfinished product that could be done better or even failure. But I do it regardless. I am so excited to share with you the principles that I have learned and applied along my journey. Despite many years of trial and error, I finally realized that it was possible to achieve the goals that I dreamed about.

My key milestones

Here are the key milestones along my journey.

1970 I was born in London, United Kingdom (U.K.).

1981 At age eleven, I started school at an all-girls boarding school in Owerri, Nigeria. I spent the next five years of my life there. My experience at this school made me who I am. This school taught me independence, strength, grit, and determination. It also taught me the importance of female camaraderie. Fetching water in buckets, scrubbing toilets, and studying with other girls was a part of my daily routine. This built a strong sense of kinship with other women.

1987 At age 17, my brother (who was 19) and I left Nigeria and returned to London to finish high school and attend college. We discovered the true meaning of hardship and the struggle to scrape by. I started my first part-time job at a 7-Eleven, and my brother started a job at an electronics store.

1989 My Mother and younger brother and sister left Nigeria and returned to London. I started college at the University of London. At the time, although I was a U.K. citizen, I did not qualify for "Home student" tuition or grants. This was because I had resided in the U.K. for less than three years. As a result, I had to pay tuition at an international student's rate.

1990 My family was unable to pay the expensive university tuition, and I had to drop out. I started working in a patisserie as an office receptionist. My small income helped at home with groceries and a couple of bills.

1991 I gained admission to study Mechanical Engineering at the University of Manchester. That time, I had been a resident for three years, so I attended tuition-free.

1993 I finally graduated college with an undergraduate degree in Mechanical Engineering. I was unable to find a job and spent a year working at a toy shop at Heathrow airport.

1994 With no employment prospects, I decided to return to graduate school. I studied for a Master's degree in Software Techniques for Computer-Aided Engineering.

1995 I graduated and started my first professional job. It was at a Computer-Aided Design software company in Coventry, U.K. I spent the next three years there. It was during this period that I realized that I most definitely did not want to continue in the field of engineering. I hated my job, and I lived for the weekends.

1998 I quit my first and only real job and returned to London where I worked as an independent contractor for two years.

2000 I landed a job at a consultant company in North Carolina and moved to the United States (U.S.). This was a difficult time for me being all alone in a new city; I didn't know anyone. I rekindled my relationship with my friend's older brother who lived in Maryland.

2001 I was laid off when the dot-com bubble burst, and I moved to Maryland to join my boyfriend.

2002 I got married, got pregnant, and started business school all in the same year. I would definitely not recommend this approach, but it worked out.

2003 I gave birth to my twins and then life took a completely new turn. Life was never the same again.

2007 I had my youngest son. That time, it was a little easier because I knew what to expect. Also, I was dealing with one newborn and not two at the same time.

Who this book is for

This book is for those of you who know that there is more to life than the way you are currently living. This book is for you if you are willing to take the step into a new way of thinking and approaching life. This book is for you if you know the status quo no longer works. You should not have to wait until your children are off to college, or until you retire to experience a full life. If you are willing to do the work that it takes to achieve your dreams, then this book is for you.

Who this book is NOT for

This book is not for you if you are looking for a get-rich-quick scheme. This book is not for you if you want overnight results. It is not for you if you are in one camp versus another: the camp that says stay-at-home Mothers make better Mothers, or the camp that says working Mothers are more ambitious. Neither camp is better than the other. We are all Mothers who work very hard every day for our families.

Please do not judge the stay-at-home Mother who is working harder than you know. Please do not judge the working Mother who is trying to juggle a family and career.

Finally, and very importantly, this book is not for you if you are not open to a faith in God. This book is faith-based. A lot of the principles that have applied to my life and to which I owe my success are because of my strong faith.

Bible Verses

Throughout the book, I reference Scripture. The Scripture I use is from the New International Version (NIV).

What you will need

You will need a notebook in which to journal as you complete the chapter exercises and write down responses to the questions. Those are included in the sections titled, "Steps to take." Later, you might also need a computer to build your own budget spreadsheet. But don't worry because the spreadsheet is simple.

The F.I.E.R.C.E Methodology by Section

I will be covering each letter in the F.I.E.R.C.E acronym within each section:

Section 1: **F**–First Things First
Section 2: **I**–I Am
Section 3: **E**–Engine
Section 4: **R**–Relationships
Section 5: **C**–Chief Financial Officer
Section 6: **E**–Execution

Section 1:
F is for First Things First

As the first letter in the F.I.E.R.C.E acronym, the letter "F" is the focus of this section.

This section on First Things First discusses the priorities of your life. What matters most to you and how should you focus your time and attention on what is most important.

As part of this section, I would like to include a celebration of Motherhood. It is important to make celebrating Motherhood a priority.

Chapter 1
Celebrating Motherhood and Celebrating You

I would like to take this first chapter to celebrate Motherhood as a calling.

Celebrating Motherhood

Mothers are F.I.E.R.C.E, awesome creatures. We hold up the skies. We produce life. And once we produce life, we are never the same again. It does not matter how young or how old our children are, they are on our minds at every moment.

We birth our children and suddenly have a Mother's instinct. That instinct would lead us to jump in front of a train without hesitation in order to save our offspring.

Short Story–"Mother going to bed"

Years ago, I came across a powerful story. In it, the anonymous author describes all the things a Mother does before she goes to bed.

Mom and Dad were watching TV when Mom said, "I'm tired and it's getting late. I think I'll go to bed."

She went to the kitchen to make sandwiches for the next day's lunches, rinsed the popcorn bowls, took meat out of the freezer for supper the following evening, checked the cereal box levels, filled the sugar container, put spoons and bowls on the table and set up the coffee pot for brewing the next morning. She then put some wet clothes into the dryer, sewed on a loose button, picked up the newspapers strewn on the floor and the game pieces left on the table and put the telephone book back into the drawer. She watered the plants, emptied a wastebasket, hung up a towel to dry, wrote a note to the teacher and counted out some cash for the kids' field trip. She signed a birthday card for a friend, addressed and stamped the envelope, and wrote a quick reminder for the grocery store. She put some water into the dog's dish and put the cat outside, then made sure the doors were locked.

Mom washed her face, put on moisturizer, and brushed and flossed her teeth. Her husband called, "I thought you were going to bed."

"I'm on my way," she replied. She looked in on each of the children, turned out a bedside lamp, hung up a shirt, threw some dirty socks in the hamper and had a brief conversation with the older one, who was up doing homework. In her own room, she set the alarm, laid out clothes for the next day, straightened up the shoe rack and added three chores to her list of things to do tomorrow.

About that time, her husband turned off the TV and announced to no one in particular, "I'm going to bed," and he did.

Of course, Fathers are amazing too in different ways. I am in no way suggesting that Mothers are better or love their children more. But, this is a book about Mothers, and I am sure there are other books that celebrate fathers.

This short story illustrates how a Mother's job is never done. We are born nurturers and make the well-being of our family our top priority. This is true of Mothers everywhere.

Celebrating you

I celebrate you. I applaud you for picking up this book. This means that you have a desire to do what it takes to crush your goals. You plan to succeed despite the daily challenges associated with being a Mother. I give you a virtual high five and walk with you as you embark on this exciting journey.

You are amazing, and I am so proud of you now, and proud of who you are about to become. You are made perfect as you are.

You have all that you need to be everything that you are born to be. You do not need to compare yourself to anyone else. You are enough, and you are made the way you intended.

All the things that you love and hate make you who you are. The things that you are good at, the things that bother you, the things that you love to do—these all comprise to make you who you are.

You are the way you are for a reason.

You are the height you are for a reason. You are the color you are for a reason. You come from the part of the world that you come from for a reason. You live where you live for a reason. You attended a particular school for a reason. You were born into the family you were born into for a reason.

Take a moment and embrace who you are with all your beauty, flaws, and personality quirks. You are amazing and if no one tells you, please know that I know you are amazing.

As we embark on this journey together, let's celebrate all that we are and all that we are created for.

If we can do this, we will stop trying to compare ourselves to anyone else. Everyone is walking along their unique and individual path on their journey. It is up to each of us to determine what path we take.

For me, success is determining what path to walk and making sure to stay on that path. For you, success may look different. But the exercises from this book will show you how to define **your** path and how to stay on it.

Chapter 2
Challenges of Motherhood

Do you agree with the following?

- Motherhood is the hardest thing that I have done.

- Motherhood is the biggest accomplishment of my life.

- Motherhood is the most rewarding thing I have ever done.

I bet you do agree. These are common sentiments brought on by Motherhood.

Nothing fills me with despair when things go wrong. Nothing else provides me with as much pride and joy when things go right. The constancy of raising my children to be strong, God-fearing, and successful, and enjoying their own journeys is all I ever need. Those are the blessings of Motherhood.

As an example, my son Ezra could not sit still in the early years, and I spent many days at school talking to teachers from pre-school through first grade. I thought, "Why can't Ezra pay attention in class?" At the time, I worried that there was something I was doing wrong. But I had faith. In the later grades, and in high school, Ezra received awards for kindness and compassion. These awards made me so proud and gave me a greater sense of pride than any of his academic achievements. Ezra may have struggled in his early years, but I know that I'm raising a son who is compassionate and kind.

Motherhood will bring you to your knees. It is the greatest calling of all, and nothing I ever achieve will come close. If I fail at raising my children to be God-fearing and successful human beings, then I have failed. My children have to stand on their own two feet when the storms of life arise. Otherwise, I have failed at everything.

One of the biggest challenges that we have as Mothers is overcoming the inability to ask for help. Often we try to do it all and end up tired, discouraged, and even resentful.

As I embarked on the journey of writing this book, my goal was to speak to all Mothers. I wanted to speak to every type of Mother at whatever stage of life you may find yourself.

I reached out to Mothers at different life stages. I wanted to learn about their biggest challenge of Motherhood. Here are some of the responses I received.

1. How to find energy when I am tired.

2. How to set the right priorities and stick to them.

3. How to assert myself and bargain for the most favorable work conditions.

4. How to be well organized for efficiency without being too rigid.

5. Why I should make time for myself and how to do that.

6. How to choose the right career path.

7. Learning from the experiences of other mothers, so I can apply their lessons learned to my own life.

8. Finding tips on how not to lose yourself.

9. Being able to accept permission to invest in my own dreams.

10. Understanding that it is never too late to achieve the life of my dreams, especially after spending many years raising my children.

11. Living my most authentic life and being a role model for my children.

12. Finding encouragement as a young mother to feel that it's okay to keep autonomy, and not only in regards to work.

13. Finding the encouragement that living the life of your dreams does not have to be all-or-nothing.

Can you relate to any of the challenges that I listed above? This is validation that you are not alone. It should be comforting to know that we are all in this together. Mothers across the globe experience some of the same challenges. These challenges exist regardless of what stage of life you may be in.

The good news is that we can tackle these challenges together. This book is one way to unite everyone through support. After all, we know that being a Mother is a meaningful and worthwhile endeavor.

Chapter 3
Purpose and Bringing It All Together

What sets your soul on fire?

If I were to ask you about that one thing that sets your soul on fire, what would be the first thing that pops into your mind?

Your children? Your marriage? Painting? Acting? Writing?

Before you had children, what would your answer have been? Would it be the same response?

You see, sometimes our life's work and the things that give us pleasure can co-exist. They are not exclusive.

Let's say you get to the end of the day. The children are finally in bed. You are finally done with work, or you have completed at least some of the tasks on your to-do list. Do you collapse on the couch and spend another two hours watching TV before going to bed? Or do you hop on your computer to start writing (or whatever activity sets your soul on fire)?

You may think it's frivolous to want to stay up all night doing what you love. This is especially true when you know you have all these other things on your to-do list. Yet, maybe writing is the one thing that gives you so much joy that you don't even notice the time flying by.

We were each born with a purpose. Our main reason is to bring our Creator glory. So, finding that purpose and pursuing it should be our life's ambition. How do we do that if we are dragging ourselves through each day only with a sense of duty or obligation?

Discovering our purpose is not hard at all. It is not a mystery that we have to uncover. We instinctively know what it is, but we may not have fully embraced it.

Our purpose sets our soul on fire. We could talk about it all day as other people's eyes glaze over. We lose track of time when we are performing a task aligned with our purpose. We think about it **all** the time. We may even dream about it while we're sleeping. I suggest keeping a small notebook and pen by your bedside and writing down some of the dreams. It can provide helpful insights.

What are you deeply troubled about?

Let's say you are going about your daily business, and you notice something. It's something that doesn't seem to bother anyone else, at least not as much as it bothers you. But it deeply bothers you. You have it at the back of your mind throughout the whole day.

Why does it have to be this way? Why can't someone fix it? Why does no one seem bothered about it?

Well, guess what—you are part of the solution!

Do you often notice something that catches your attention? When this happens, do you start thinking about ways to make it better without even realizing it? You think to yourself, "This is lovely, but if it had xyz, it would be fantastic."

When you daydream, what do you dream about doing?

Bear in mind that it may not be one thing; it could be several things.

What are the things that you could talk about for a long time? Do these subjects trigger you to launch into a diatribe or long discussion with passion?

That is a big clue about your purpose.

Since I was little, I had a strong desire to build a school and home for children. I was particularly drawn to children in the range of newborns to the age of about ten. I remember the first time I visited an orphanage in Nigeria. I was nine or ten years old at the time.

I remember thinking that my life's work would be to help disadvantaged children in some fashion. This was something that deeply troubled me and although people around me felt it was sad, I did not understand why no one else seemed to be as deeply affected by this as I did.

The thought of young children in distress turns me inside out. My desire to help never left, and I have found ways to incorporate that passion into my daily life.

I partner with a nonprofit to help disadvantaged children in Eastern Nigeria. I also sponsor ten-year-old twins in Haiti. I try to go on a mission trip to Nigeria or Haiti every year to volunteer and work with these children. When I ran the New York Marathon for the second time, I raised money for an organization working with children in South Africa.

It is important to note that we may be part of a solution, but we will likely be unable to fix the problem. Keeping this in mind will help reduce the feeling of overwhelm. We are not called to solve all the problems of the world.

Instead, we can make genuine efforts to help as best as we can.

What makes you excited to get out of bed?

What would you be doing with your life that would make you leap out of bed each day with excitement?

Please do not look at your current situation and think that's impossible without all of your responsibilities.

Just dream with me for a minute. What would make you super excited to start the day?

Before you close your eyes at night, what would make you think to yourself, "I can't wait to wake up and get going so I can do X?"

Then, you wake up in the morning and your eyes fly open. Mornings become the best part of your day. Gone are the days of rude alarm clock awakenings, groaning, and hitting the snooze button.

Instead, you wake up refreshed, excited, and ready to go. What would that look like?

What is that X factor that you could spend all day doing?

As we journey through this book, try to keep this question in mind, "How can I change my life so that I am excited to get out of bed each morning?"

We will spend time setting realistic goals to guide you along the path to achieving a positive life change.

I have been working on it too, and I am excited to go on this journey with you.

What comes easily to you?

Does anyone ask what comes easily to you? This question makes me chuckle. Nothing comes easily to me. I feel like with everything I attempt to do, I struggle and have to work hard.

When I look around, I am in awe of people that can sing, people that can act, people that absorb information quickly, and people that can perform a task ten times faster than I ever could. I really do not believe that anything comes easily to me.

But there is another way to think about this. What would your close friends say if they were asked what you are really good at doing?

When they respond, you may think, "I am not that good at this thing," or "It is no big deal, anyone could do that." That "no-big-deal" thinking is exactly what I am getting at.

If it is not a big deal to you, and you think everyone can do it, it is because it is easy (or at least easier) for you to do that thing compared to everyone else.

That seemingly easy thing can provide another clue that points to your purpose.

As an example, I am pretty organized and planning tasks makes me excited. I tend to find it easy to plan things out and make lists. I am usually put in charge of organizing events and making sure things go according to plan. Planning is not too big of a deal to me, but some people struggle with it.

Your purpose is not something that is so difficult for you that it causes you distress or makes you struggle to achieve it. Of course, the journey to fulfilling our purpose in life will have challenges and will be very intimidating at times. But we are given the unique capabilities and talent to perform our purpose—we are given certain abilities that others are not. Those other people may be able to perform a task well but with greater difficulty and at a slower pace. Do not take your abilities for granted. It is worth taking some time to figure out what you are really good at.

Steps to take

Take out your journal and write the responses to the following prompts.

1. What is the first thing that pops into your head when I ask, "What sets your soul on fire?" Don't worry about what it is. Just write down the very first thing that comes to mind.

2. If you could do anything in the world and money was no object, what would you be doing? Could you do this for the rest of your life? Where would you live? What location, what type of house? By the water? In the countryside? Would you retire to Florida? Be sure to write all of this down too.

3. How would you spend your days? Plan out the perfect day. A day in the life of you, or a life in the day of you, depending on how you think about it. Write this all down.

4. What are your hobbies? What do you love to do for fun? Use this opportunity to list any hobbies or favorite activities that you have.

5. List your top five pet peeves in order of most irritating to least irritating.

6. Name that one thing that would cause you to leap out of bed with excitement. It should be the thing that if it could become your job, you would be happy to do every day.

7. What do you think that you are pretty good at that you take for granted? Take a few minutes to think about this. You may try to disregard that talent or interest because it seems like no big deal to you. You may notice that others struggle with that same thing, but you think nothing of it.

In the next chapter, we discuss how to leave a lasting legacy. This is something that tells the world that we once walked the face of the earth.

Chapter 4
Leaving a Legacy

Be intentional

Some people know exactly what they want to do from the moment that they are little. They have an immediate response to, "When I grow up I want to be ___."

Most of us have no clue. I had no idea, and I often say that for someone who had no idea what she wanted to do with her life, I have not done too badly.

But we are only on earth for a set length of time. How do we make it count?

What does it mean to leave a legacy for the next generation? This has nothing to do with how much money we make. It has nothing to do with the size of our houses or the labels in our closet. Leaving a legacy is about becoming a successful role model for the younger generations.

So how can we be successful role models for our children and for younger people who may (or may not) look up to us?

My heart's desire is for my children to be able to stand strong in this world because of the example I have set for them.

My actions, my living life with intention, will point my children in the right direction.

I pray for the same thing for you—a life of intention to guide your children in the right direction.

That will leave a strong legacy for our children.

Life is a gift as hard and challenging as it can be. If we view each day as a gift, we can be intentional about everything we do. What will I do with this gift that many did not receive? What will I do with this day that is full of possibilities? How will I make this day an adventure?

Each day lived with intention will add up to a lifetime of legacy. A lifetime of legacy is something that we can leave for the next generation.

Giving back

Time

As I get older, I realize that time is the most precious resource that I have. We are all given 24 hours a day, and for most of us, that is not enough. God in His infinite wisdom gave us limited hours each day. He also gave us free will to choose how we spend that time.

Here are a few ways we spend our time:

- Sleep

- Eating

- Work

- Childrens' activities

- Managing a household

- Helping children with homework

- Preparing meals

- Traveling to and from work

- Exercise

Let's look at dividing that time out by the approximate time it takes for each activity:

- Sleep – 6 hours

- Eating – 0.5 hour

- Work – 8 hours

- Childrens' activities – 1 hour

- Managing a household – 2 hours

- Helping children with homework – 1 hour

- Preparing meals – 1 hour

- Traveling to and from work – 1.5 hours

- Exercise – 1 hour

That only leaves two hours each day for downtime. I know I have missed several other tasks that are equally as important as the tasks that I listed above.

My point is—where do we have time for anything extra? This is why God values the time that we spend with Him and working on the things on which He places value. He understands how precious our time is.

This is why to walk in our purpose—time management is so critical.

I have found that the best solution to the time management challenge is for me to plan. I have a weekly and daily schedule where I map out everything that I have to do, by the hour. I know this sounds rigid, and I do leave a little room for the unexpected. It has helped relieve a lot of the stress that I have related to the restrictions of a typical day.

My plan looks something like this:

5 a.m. – Wake up and prayer time

5:45 a.m. – Wake the children

5:45–6:45 a.m. – Support the children as they get ready for school

6:45 a.m. – Drop children at the train station

7–8 a.m. – Work out

8 a.m. – Get ready for work

8:30 a.m. – Start work

6 p.m. – Family dinner (Prep and eat)

7–9 p.m. – Focus on goals

9–9:30 p.m. – Downtime to laugh and chat with my husband if he is home

9:30 p.m. – Bedtime

My children are older so they are more independent and their activities take place at school. So, this schedule may look different for you, especially if you have younger children, or if you work from home. But, it will give you an idea of how you can plan out your day and reduce stress. Each day is different and life doesn't always stick to a plan, but I use this as a general approach.

Talent

The dictionary defines talent as an aptitude or skill for a group of activities.

We all have a natural aptitude for something.

To whom much is given, much is expected. One of the major ways we can give back is to donate our talents.

I used to think that talent was something that was reserved for famous people. I thought they became famous because they were so good at something. A few examples of famous individuals and their talents are:

- Whitney Houston's voice

- Michael Jordan's basketball skills

- Martin Luther King, Jr. and his oratory skills

- Tiger Woods and his golf skills

I thought, "I could not have any kind of talent because I am neither rich nor famous."

Yet, talent is much simpler than that. We are all talented. The world may not realize it, but we all have our own talent. Hopefully you've been able to identify your talent through the previous writing exercises.

But how do we contribute our talents to the world? We can incorporate our talents into some kind of service to those around us. This could be the type of work you do if you work outside the home. Or, perhaps finding some way to help someone else. Are you good with numbers? Perhaps you could help a friend create a budget. Your talent doesn't always result in financial gain. It is more important to volunteer or support others by using your talents.

Treasure

It is impossible to save the whole world. The Bible tells us that the poor will always exist.

Yet, it is important to know that we have a responsibility to impact our world for good. To whom much is given, much is expected.

We are expected to give, but giving alone is not enough. The heart in which we give is as important.

2 Corinthians 9:7 says, "Each of you should give what you have decided in your heart to give, not reluctantly or under compulsion, for God loves a cheerful giver."

My goal here is not to make you feel guilty. My goal is to encourage you to consider supporting a charitable organization. Or, help the less fortunate in some way that uses your talents. Doing so will help to take our minds off our own struggles by putting things in perspective.

Steps to take

Write in your journal to respond to each of the following.

1. How might trusting God as the source of your life change your outlook and change the way you approach each day? Write down what this would look like.

2. Think about ways you can find some time to spend with God each day.

3. Consider how you may help make an impact on the world by giving your time, talent, or treasure. Please remember that this is not an all-or-nothing approach. It may be completely impractical to volunteer for a few hours a week for an organization. Yet, it may be possible to pick a charity of your choice to support in another way. You could become a sponsor for a nonprofit that does work that you are passionate about and/or make a small monthly pledge.

In this chapter, we looked at simple ways to leave your legacy by making your contribution to the world. Being a role model for the next generation and using your time, talent, and treasure is the greatest way to leave your legacy.

In the next chapter, we discuss Motherhood. I would like to celebrate Motherhood and give you a chance to pat yourself on the back.

I will give you the opportunity to remember specific tales from the trenches, and I share some of my own memories.

Chapter 5
Motherhood

Mothers, we are amazing creatures. We birthed life, and we work hard every day to ensure our children are thriving and have all that they need. It is easy to say that we are not given a Mother's instruction manual, but actually we are.

We are not called to be perfect Mothers, but we are called to trust God with the precious gifts that we are given.

As a Christian Mother, I understand that my children do not belong to me. They were given to me as a gift to steward.

There is nothing that concerns my children that does not concern God. He is aware of every situation they will ever face.

I have also come to understand that God loves my children more than I do. What an incredible blessing even though I'm unsure how it's possible.

Admiring everything about our children

We're all proud of our children. Can I take a moment to brag about mine? When you read this, I would like you to think of the ways that you can brag about your own children.

Each of my three children is so different. I have twins (a boy and a girl) who are 16, and my youngest (boy) who is 12.

My oldest son Ezra is quiet, introverted, and quirky. He has such a strong sense of who he is and has no desire to conform to what everyone else is doing. He has a very set view of how things should be and will not bend. Of all my three children, he used to be the one I worried about the most.

Ezra has such a kind heart. He hates to see anyone in pain and will swoop in to help in an instant. I will never forget how on a long haul flight he sat next to a younger boy who was in tears and was traveling alone. Ezra swapped seats with this boy because his TV was not working. He wanted to cheer up the boy. I know what a sacrifice this was for Ezra because he loves to watch movies on long haul flights. He could not bear to see this boy upset.

Azure is my only daughter and Ezra's twin. She is my mini-me. She looks a lot like me and has a few similarities. She is serious-minded, ambitious, driven, and eager to please. I love the young lady that she is. I love having a daughter, and we are very close. I am so grateful to be her Mother. She is my energizer bunny and my high achiever.

She rows varsity crew for her high school, which involves leaving the house at 4:30 a.m. to get to the water. We live quite a distance from her rowing location. So, the early morning drive is a great way for us to connect and catch up on what is going on in her life. She loves to row and has become quite a strong rower. She wants to row in college and spends a lot of time staying in rowing shape. She eats the right foods to fuel her in the right way. I am so proud of her.

Noah is the baby of the family. He is my scrappy, streetwise child. He has grown up defending himself from his older siblings. So, he is sharp-witted and ready to fight for what he wants. He is the most affectionate of my children, though, and loves to snuggle and have his bedtime stories read to him. When he was younger, he would demand a different story every night. It had to be a story that I would make up on the spot. When I finished the story, he would rate the quality of the story on a scale of one to ten. He makes me laugh a lot. He is earnest, serious, mischievous, and funny all at the same time. At age six, he announced that he wanted to be president someday. He changed his mind in 2015 after watching one of the presidential debates. He declared that it was "too much work."

All three of my children are introverts, like their parents, but to different degrees.

My youngest is the least introverted. My daughter is a close second, and my oldest son is the most introverted.

He coined the phrase "socially exhausted" after spending an evening out with friends.

The reason that I describe each child in some detail is to show you how different each child is. I cannot apply a one-size-fits-all approach to parenting, it just would not work. Being the amazing creatures that we are, Mothers have that innate ability to discern the differences in each child and parent each child based on their differences.

In the grand scheme of things, Motherhood has been and is the most important calling for me. I will be measured as a Mother first, but it is not the only thing I will be measured on. Similarly, you may have identified another calling to write a book, start a side business, etc. Just remember that despite Motherhood being the ultimate calling, it's also important to live a full life of purpose and to do the other things that you know you are uniquely able to do.

No one is doing it right

I always knew that I wanted to be a Mother. I always knew that I wanted to have three children. I always knew that I wanted to have twins. I always knew that I wanted to have two boys and a girl. The only minor detail that did not go as expected, is that I thought that I would have twin boys and a younger girl. But I ended up having boy-girl twins and a younger boy, and I'm so thankful.

I love being a Mother. It is the biggest accomplishment of my life. At the end of it all, nothing will be worth achieving if I fail to raise my children the right way.

I used to be a hardworking overwhelmed Mother who felt like I could not get to the next level. I felt tired all the time and could not find enough hours in the day to focus on my goals. I also felt like there was never enough money, and I lived paycheck to paycheck.

I wanted to be able to have it all. I wanted to be a successful Mother, engaged in raising my children, while also achieving everything at work and reaching my personal goals.

I worked such long hours, and I traveled a lot with work, so I felt like I was missing out on my childrens' lives.

I wanted the respect of those closest to me, and I did not want to show any weaknesses.

I was not doing particularly well in either my career or home life. I was definitely on the "Mommy track" at work, and I often felt sad. Things did eventually change with time. I learned to be patient and not to be so hard on myself. I also learned to admit when I needed help and allow other people to help too.

I remember a particularly painful moment after returning from one of my work trips. I came up the stairs, and the babysitter was carrying my son who was one and a half years old at the time. I went to carry him, and he refused to let me carry him. Can you imagine how I felt?

Can you relate to how I was feeling? You may be feeling that way now. Perhaps you feel that you are unable to do anything well. You are juggling so many responsibilities that you feel like you cannot give each one your full attention. I can relate to everything you are feeling.

Do you feel like everyone else has it together, and you are just dragging yourself through each day?

Do you have dreams that you have put on hold because, well, "I am a Mommy now"? Do you feel as if you have to pick up the slack at home and still have to perform on the job?

I can relate to how you feel.

It is important to understand that none of us are doing Motherhood perfectly. I love the expression "Do it ugly." We as Mothers show up every day with all of our imperfections, and we do what we can.

So how do we measure success as a Mother? How do we know whether we are doing it right? Do we never find out until it is all done with? Or, do we see evidence of our successful parenting along the way?

I was in the car with my teenage daughter a couple of months ago, and we were chatting about something. I don't even remember what it was. In response to something that I said, she exclaimed, "Honestly, I don't think anyone knows what they are doing." Instinctively, I yelled, "Hello?!" It was so profound and on point.

Is that not the truth? We look great on the outside, but inside we are truly figuring it all out as we go along. And that is okay.

Tales from the trenches

In raising our children, each in our own way in what we believe is right, we have tales from the trenches.

When my daughter was in kindergarten, she got head lice from another girl at school.

My daughter had very thick hair, and we did not detect this for months. Of course, everyone else in the house caught it too, except my husband who is bald. It took us three years (yes, three years) to get rid of the lice completely.

I shaved my head several times, and as soon as I would start to grow a little hair, I would feel the itch.

I thought I would lose my mind.

We tried every lotion, home remedy, and trick on the planet. I can chuckle now at some of the things we tried. One remedy was to put fresh rosemary on the pillows. The smell would cause the head lice to crawl out of the scalp and onto the pillow. Well, I do not need to tell you how well that worked.

After a couple of years, I came across an advertisement for a dry, heated air contraption. The advertisement claimed to eliminate the lice by rendering the females infertile. It did not kill the lice, but they were no longer able to lay any eggs. Also, the ad claimed that the dry heat from this machine would prevent the eggs that already existed from hatching. I had nothing to lose.

It sounded crazy, but it worked. I cannot begin to explain the relief. After close to three years, we began to accept head lice as a way of life. I even ended up in the hospital, which is actually how I found out that I am most allergic to sulfa drugs.

I had read online that Bactrim (the sulfa-based antibiotic) was effective in eliminating head lice. My daughter had some left in a bottle that we had previously used to treat a skin fungus (that's another story). So, I took the Bactrim.

My eyes turned bloodshot red, and I was so ill, I had to take myself to the ER. My husband was out of town. Luckily, a friend of mine was staying with us and accompanied me.

Why do I tell you this horrifying story? I tell you this because it is a tale from the trenches. And I know you have tales from the trenches too.

This experience taught me that it is impossible to escape Motherhood without a challenging experience. It taught me to embrace the rough times and learn what I can. Also, it's important to express gratitude during the easy times.

These experiences become the stories that we recant to each other when the children are grown. They become memories that we hope to one day tell our grandchildren.

Steps to take

Use your journal to record your thoughts about the following questions.

1. Take a few minutes to write about each of your children. Talk about their unique personalities. Chuckle to yourself about the things that each child does to make you laugh.

2. Celebrate each child. Celebrate their uniqueness and their accomplishments. For example, my daughter loves verbal affirmations. My sons prefer rewards of some kind, like a trip to their favorite restaurant. Once you know what each child responds to, celebrate them in the way that they will most appreciate.

3. What tales from the trenches can you remember? Write down one story. What happened? How did you react? How did the experience shape you? What did you learn from the experience? If you had to go through it again, what would you do differently? How can you help someone else who may be going through a similar experience?

In the next chapter, I discuss careers and work. We are all working Mothers, some of us work in the home, and some work for an outside organization. Either way, we all work. And we work very hard.

My experiences are based on my time in corporate America. I have worked in the corporate world for the last fifteen years, so I share my advice from that perspective. The experiences gave me valuable life lessons.

Chapter 6
Careers and Work

Mothers in the workforce

As Mothers, we all work super hard whether we work at home or at a job.

I write from the experience of a Mother working outside of the home. Being a Mother in the workforce has not been easy. It has been challenging to balance all responsibilities and not be able to volunteer at school as much as I would like. I did make sure to be in the Parent Association and attend as many meetings as possible to keep abreast of what was happening at the school.

But I've always felt that I was not able to give my all. I felt guilty while at work because I was not at home. At home, I felt like I was missing deadlines and not performing at my full work potential.

There was never a day that I felt that I had accomplished everything. Someone would always have to sacrifice something. I did my best not to miss any plays, rehearsals, and parent-teacher meetings, but this was not always possible. Thankfully my husband would step in to attend whenever I was unable.

My children learned from an early age to be independent. They were able to self-manage and organize their schedules as much as was possible for their age. They learned to plan ahead and know when projects and assignments were due, and to make sure field trip forms were signed in a timely fashion.

I was never one of those Mothers that baked cupcakes for the school bake sale. Instead, I knew where the closest grocery stores or Dunkin' Donuts stores were.

Despite all of that, my children knew I loved them. They knew that they could tell me anything. They knew I would be there for them even though I could not always be physically present.

It has gotten a lot easier, particularly because I do not travel as much as I used to, and I work remotely from home.

But I am always working—on a conference call, rushing to get a presentation done, or creating a financial model.

The children know that they can walk into my office at any moment. They can ask something, and I would be available to answer.

For the Mothers that stay at home, it is nice to be in the home and available for your children when they have questions or need something. Your challenges may be different from mine. For example, you may feel that you never get a chance to do something for yourself.

All Mothers are spread pretty thin. It's important to prioritize self-care and learn to ask for help.

Speaking up

It is important to speak up and clearly explain expectations and what is feasible. As an example of why we should speak up, I'll share a story from work.

My job involves working with numbers. I work in spreadsheets for a majority of my day. I then create presentations from the spreadsheet analyses.

I say this to explain that in my line of work, it is easy to make mistakes when you are running at a hundred miles per hour. Attention to detail is critical because a small mistake has a huge impact.

Recently, the account team and I had been working on a large deal for a potential customer. There were a lot of eyes on this deal at the executive level. The account team was running at a fast pace to close the deal.

I had to create a financial analysis. It needed to explain why the potential customer would benefit from our solution.

The first mistake that I made was not speaking up. I should have sounded the alarm that the turnaround time was too short to do a careful analysis. I was tasked with getting the presentation to the customer on Friday, and it was Wednesday. There was not enough time to complete a proper analysis and create a quality presentation.

Instead, I told the account team that although the timing was tight, I could get my part done.

Needless to say, I worked late and through the day on Friday for a 7 p.m. meeting with the customer.

I had worked so hard on this presentation, especially considering the limited time frame.

A few slides into the presentation, the customer started to notice errors. Some of the inputs that they had provided to us were wrong.

I made an effort to reassure the customer. I told them that the story was the same, and I would correct the errors. I did not realize that the customer was not convinced.

Later, the feedback we received from the customer was that my presentation was a mess. There are no words to explain how I felt after that. I had been doing this line of work for over 15 years. I still had a huge amount to learn, but it was the first time I had ever received such a terrible customer review.

There are many lessons I learned from this experience, and I list them below:

1. **Fall on your sword fast.** I did not try to cover my tracks or blame anyone else. I owned up to the account team right away that I had made these errors.

2. **Speak up.** If a deadline seems unreasonable to you, say so. It is better to set expectations and force a slower pace to create quality work. The alternative is to rush a project to please people and end up jeopardizing the whole project.

3. **Take stock.** What are some of the reasons that the mistake happened? In this instance, I had been working late and not getting enough sleep. I had been burning the candle at both ends. The

poor quality of my work had an impact on everyone involved in the project.

4. **Forgive yourself and move on.** I beat myself up hard, and I felt so bad for a while. This continued until I realized that I could not move on until I forgave myself. It would not be the last time that I would make a mistake. But I would not be making that same mistake again.

I tell this story because we all make mistakes, albeit some are bigger than others. It is important to remember that no one is immune to mistakes, especially when Mothers are used to being pulled in so many directions. The goal is to learn from your mistakes and course correct to avoid the same mistake in the future.

I have many stories from working in corporate America—some are stories of triumph and victory, some are stories of defeat.

I know what the never-ending to-do list feels like; it's even worse when coupled with the sheer exhaustion of being a Mother. I have cried many tears and felt like I was never good enough. I have mastered the plastered smile despite the tears welling up. If you have had some of the same experiences, then I know exactly how you feel. I have been there.

If I can encourage you, I will say it does get easier in a sense. You will become tougher and smarter about speaking up and enlisting help when you need it.

A seat at the table

I am talking in the context of working Mothers, but I believe that these tips will help Mothers in general. How do you earn a seat at a table? How do you get to the point in your career or life where people listen to what you have to say?

It does not happen overnight. I have been working in corporate America for over fifteen years, and I can confirm that it takes time and patience to get to that point where you're heard.

I'm still working on it. For every step that you reach, there are still steps ahead.

Here are some of the things that have helped me thus far. Admittedly, I am still a work in progress with regard to many of the items on this list.

1. **Show up on time.** If you are late, it shows a lack of reliability.

2. **Learn to say yes.** Raise your hand for projects that will help you to showcase your skills and strengths. (Just don't say yes to so much that you overcommit.)

3. **Do what you say you will do.** Do not commit to something that you know you are unable to deliver. If you say you will have a deliverable completed by a certain date, have it completed. Excuses don't work very well in a corporate environment.

4. **Speak up.** Do not be afraid to articulate your point of view.

5. **Make sure that your work is of the highest quality possible.** We could all do a better job in this area, and I am always working to improve the quality of my work.

6. **Be pleasant.** People gravitate toward people that they like. Show up with a smile. Remember the little things about people that others may forget.

7. **Actively listen.** This means that you listen intently without the intention of responding right away.

8. **Ask probing questions.** Be honest if you do not understand something. Clarity about the tasks helps with focus.

9. **Be known for something.** Are you a good presenter? Are you a great facilitator? Do you have excellent writing skills? Are you always on time? If a task comes up that's to your talent, work hard to apply your skill and be the first person on people's minds.

10. **Get a sponsor and a mentor.** A mentor is someone that can guide you along your career path. A mentor will share their experiences and help you set career goals. A sponsor takes it even further. A career sponsor is someone with authority who can speak on your behalf when you are not in the room. See my takeaway from my podcast interview with Dr. Adaeze Enekwechi in the bonus section. In this episode, Dr. Enekwechi covers the topic of career sponsors in great detail.

In the next section, we focus on the "**I**" **for I am.** This section is a critical piece of the puzzle as it will uncover current mindsets. This section will explain why having the right mindset is the key to accomplishing goals.

Let's have some fun discovering who we are and what makes us so qualified to accomplish our goals. We already have the qualifications to live a life of purpose.

Section 2:
I is for I Am

Chapter 7
Mindset and Motivation

In this chapter, we talk about mindset and motivation. We look at this concept from different angles. We will ask ourselves:

- What is my why?

- What will keep me going when things get hard?

- What will I do when I want to give up?

This chapter covers the principle of visualization. We discuss ways to visualize the future that we are dreaming about. We need to remind ourselves that we are built of tough material. We can keep going when things get tough. We can do hard things. We define determination and strategies to stay focused.

The chapter wouldn't be complete if we did not identify some of the limiting beliefs that we have. These limiting beliefs may be conscious or unconscious. These are some of the things that we tell ourselves that hinder our progress and make it easier to give up or quit. **Recognizing those limitations gives you power.**

What is your why?

What do you want to accomplish? Why do you want to accomplish that goal? Define it and your hard work will always be worth achieving.

How do you define your why? Let's define what you want to achieve. We will call this goal "it."

1. What do you want to achieve?

2. For whom do you want to achieve it?

3. How do you think you will feel when you achieve it?

4. What will you do when you achieve it?

5. How will you keep going when every fiber of your being is screaming at you to quit?

6. What do you think will prevent you from achieving it?

7. What skills do you need to achieve it?

8. How hard will you have to work to achieve it?

9. What will you have to sacrifice to achieve it?

10. What strengths do you have, that you believe will come in handy on your journey?

11. What mindset corrections do you need to make?

Whenever you feel like giving up, come back to this section. Remind yourself why and for whom you are doing this. It will remind you why you are putting yourself through this process.

You can do hard things

Philippians 4:13 says, "I can do all this through him who gives me strength."

You can do hard things. Have you ever looked back on a time in your life and thought to yourself, "I don't know how I got through that period?" or "I don't know how I was able to do XYZ?".

We all have those moments when we wonder how we survived a tough a period of our lives. But we can do hard things. We are built to last. We are built to endure. We are made of quality material. We may bend, but we do not easily break.

If you and I get discouraged (as Mothers we often do), we should remind ourselves that we can do hard things. We have done it before. It was tough. We can't believe that we went through it, but we can do it again, and again, and again.

As long as we keep our engines humming, and our machines maintained, we are built to last. I devote "Section 3 – E is for Engine" to the ways we can maintain our engine and do self-care. We have to keep our engines humming!

Psalm 18:23 says, "By my God, I can run through a troop and leap over a wall."

That sounds pretty fierce to me. I can do hard things. I am stronger than I know. Say it with me!

Determination

The Cambridge dictionary defines determination as "the ability to continue trying to do something, although it is very difficult."

I love the following verse of Scripture. It always comes to my mind when I think about determination. It speaks to the fact that you cannot be determined unless you believe that success is assured.

Isaiah 50:7 says, "Because the Sovereign Lord helps me, I will not be disgraced. Therefore have I set my face like flint, and I know I will not be put to shame."

What does it mean to set one's face as flint?

It implies some kind of preparation for adversity or opposition. You know there will be challenges ahead, but you can prepare.

Setting one's face like flint means putting your game face on, or to take on a serious disposition. You are ready to go to war and be victorious over the opposition.

As a Christian, I can put my game face on because I know that the Lord will help me, just as it says in **Isaiah 50:7.**

We need to start the journey with determination, with our game face on, ready to face the challenges ahead.

Determination is critical to success. It is what will see you through when the going gets rough. And trust me, the going will get rough.

Do not struggle alone

It may seem like I am contradicting myself based on everything I said in the previous paragraph. But, if you are struggling, please do not struggle alone.

You know deep down whether a struggle is a temporary situation. You may just need a kick in the behind or motivation. Or, the way you are feeling may be indicative of a bigger problem.

Are you are struggling to get through the day? Does the simplest of tasks make it seem like you are climbing a mountain with no pinnacle? Then please do not be too hard on yourself or feel like you should be doing a better job with life.

We all need help sometimes. Sometimes we need someone to take over for a little bit while we lie in bed.

Oftentimes, the reality is that person does not exist. So, we struggle under the heaviness of our burden.

Here is a list of resources that may prove helpful as a start. It is not an exhaustive list, but will help you get started:

1. Substance Abuse and Mental Health Services Administration—**1-800-662-HELP (4357)** https://www.samhsa.gov/find-help/national-helpline

2. National Institute of Mental Health— https://www.nimh.nih.gov

3. MentalHealth.gov— https://www.mentalhealth.gov

I am not a mental health professional and will not attempt to feign any kind of expertise in this area. But, there are many resources available to help when you and I are not feeling well. You owe it to yourself to pick up the phone and call. You owe it to your children. You owe it to the future you. Because in reality, you're already crushing it.

Life can wear us down and situations and circumstances can knock the wind out of us.

Getting help when you are struggling is a major first step to creating the life that you desire. Do not tell yourself to suck it up when you know that it is deeper than that. Please don't ignore the problem.

I applaud you for taking the next step toward improving your mental health. I am cheering for you! I am reaching through the pages and holding your hands and saying, "Girl, you can do this. I am cheering from the sidelines. It will get better. You can get better."

Limiting beliefs

Let's talk about limiting beliefs. A limiting belief is a lie that we have accepted about ourselves. This lie is preventing us from taking a leap into the unknown. The unknown could be applying for a new job. It could be asking for a raise or a promotion. It may be starting a new business or starting an exercise program to improve your health.

A limiting belief will prevent you from living your best life.

We all have them. I am working to overcome a long list of limiting beliefs.

My biggest limiting belief is that the world, particularly the online world, is a crowded and noisy place. It seems like everyone is creating a podcast, writing a book, or selling an online course.

I have told myself that no one cares what a close to 50-year-old woman has to say. I have told myself that I would be adding to the already noisy marketplace.

My biggest limiting belief is that I am too old. I should leave things to the "youngsters."

The funny thing about a limiting belief is that we are aware of it, and we know deep down that it is not true. There are a lot of people in the world that are a lot older than me and have started successful ventures. Why should it be any different for me?

Besides, the limiting belief usually stems from insecurity. The biggest question we ask ourselves is, "What if I fail?" You ask yourself, "What will people think of me?" And you think, "Oh, the embarrassment would be terrible if I don't become a mega success overnight."

I have found a method which has proven to be successful in overcoming a limiting belief.

The questions I ask myself when my limiting beliefs rear their ugly heads is "So what if you fail? Who cares?" The same people you claim are not interested in what you have to say are too busy. They are too busy worrying about what everyone else is thinking about them. They are too busy to care.

The second question I ask myself is "What do you have to lose?" Really, though, what is the worst thing that can happen?

For example, I may speak to myself and say, "Your Mother is the only person that will buy your book." That is the worst-case scenario. So, what happens if that is the reality? Then what?

Thinking about the worst that could happen and embracing it helps to minimize the fear of the unknown. This has been my experience. I believe the reason it works is because whatever happens, it will be better than my worst-case scenario. My Mother, my husband, my siblings, and my close friends will buy my book. That is at least twenty people. I would not call that a mega success, but it is twenty times better than my worst-case scenario. Do you see where I am going?

You and I need to throw caution to the wind (within reason) and take the leap.

What is the worst that can happen?

Steps to take

In your journal, write your responses to the following questions.

Determination

1. What are you determined to do? What do you need determination for?

2. We will not be setting goals yet. We will get to that later. But I would like you to resolve that no matter how hard it gets, you will stick it out. You will commit to achieving your goals. You will suck it up when it gets hard. You will "gut" it out. My running coach a few years ago would use this phrase on the long runs, when the group started to get tired. This means that you will not give up. Instead, you will settle in for the tough journey ahead and dig deep for strength. Write down your promise to yourself.

Limiting Beliefs

1. Take a few minutes to list your limiting beliefs. Write as many of them down that you can think of.

2. Before you go to the next chapter, address each limiting belief with a "So what?" response. Write your imagined worst-case scenario beside each one. Embrace the fear knowing that the reality will always be better. Then move onto the next limiting belief.

3. Put the list somewhere that you can see it regularly. It will remind you that you can strive for what you previously thought was unachievable.

Please do not move on to the next chapter until you have gone through these exercises.

In the next chapter, we work on self-affirmations and the words that we speak to ourselves. This is a follow up from the work we have done in this chapter. We will be tackling our limiting beliefs so we can move forward and accomplish our unique purpose.

Chapter 8
Affirmations

Twenty things

I went to an event recently that my friend Kwavi facilitated for ladies. As part of that event, she gave us an exercise.

The exercise was to come up with twenty things that you love about yourself. She gave us three minutes to complete this exercise.

I was able to come up with fourteen on the first attempt. I was surprised that I was not able to come up with twenty. But when I recognized that if I went easy on myself, I was doing a lot better than before.

The funny thing about this exercise is that we do not have to share the results with anyone else. Yet, we may still feel uncomfortable listing the things that make us so great.

It can be a struggle for us women to affirm ourselves. It can seem conceited and arrogant to come up with things that we love about ourselves. But this is a very important exercise because it teaches us to love ourselves more. We cannot give what we do not have. And if we do not love ourselves, how can we love others?

How would friends describe me?

A helpful alternative exercise is to consider the question "How would my friends describe me?"

This is an important question to ask. It will shed light on areas of our personalities that we may not be aware of.

If someone were to ask me what five qualities my friends would use to describe me, I would say the following:

1. Strong

2. Quiet

3. Determined

4. Stubborn

5. Hardworking

It is interesting that I list these qualities. I have not confirmed these five qualities with my friends, nor do I need to. This is an important exercise in self-awareness, and the exercise offers us insight that we are often harder on ourselves than we should be.

Self-amplification

The Oxford Dictionary defines **self-promotion** as "the action of promoting or publicizing oneself or one's activities, especially in a forceful way." The example the dictionary gives is:

"She's guilty of criminally bad taste and shameless self-promotion."

If you read this, you would not be blamed at all for thinking that self-promotion is a bad thing. It appears to be self-serving, conceited, and arrogant.

But I would like us to look at this concept in a different light.

Self-promotion, at the very least, is a form of self-preservation or survival. It is a way of highlighting your accomplishments. It's important because these accomplishments may otherwise go unrecognized.

Self-promotion is a way of advocating for yourself. You should speak up for yourself when others may be unwilling to do so or when others do not see what you would like them to see.

Self-promotion may seem more important for your career and in the workplace. But it holds great importance in other areas of life too.

Self-promotion is not a way of bragging. Instead, think of it as a way of sharing ideas and skills to help move our purpose forward. It is a vital skill to have when done the right way.

Self-promotion is difficult for women. As Mothers, we are comfortable and accustomed to putting everyone else first. So, we may struggle to come up with anything about ourselves worth promoting. Once we do this, we then have to overcome the challenge of promoting ourselves.

Whatever you do, please do not put yourself down. You should never speak to yourself in a way that you would not tolerate for your loved ones. Learn to catch yourself and silence your inner bully.

Every time you catch yourself thinking something that is self-derogatory, say something positive to yourself that cancels this out. I do this all the time. For example, I may catch myself saying "How could you be so stupid,

Ugochi?" I will immediately stop and say, "I am not stupid. I may have made a mistake, but I am not stupid. I am smart and I resolve to be more careful."

#IamRemarkable

I recently attended a session at work called #IamRemarkable.

#IamRemarkable is a Google initiative. It empowers women and underrepresented groups to celebrate their achievements in the workplace and beyond. For more information about the #IamRemarkable initiative, please visit the website: https://iamremarkable.withgoogle.com.

The goal of the #IamRemarkable initiative is to improve the self-promotion of women and underrepresented groups and to motivate these individuals to promote themselves.

In this session, we were asked to challenge the social perception around self-promotion. Everyone in the session had to complete two tasks.

The first task was to write a list of all personal accomplishments that came to mind.

The second task was to divide into groups and read out one accomplishment on the list. This would be the one thing that we wanted to share with the group.

Even with the permission of the facilitator to self-promote, this was an incredibly tough task. It was difficult because I am not used to this behavior. I have always believed that self-promotion is proud or arrogant and that I am boasting when I say something that is self-promoting. I was not the only one struggling either. A lot of other people in the room shared that they found this exercise difficult too.

If you notice, throughout this book, I encourage you to pause and take an inventory of how great you are.

The purpose is not to make you feel good about yourself and to make you feel happy that you read this book.

The self-inventory serves a greater purpose. We need to understand as individuals, and as Mothers, how incredible we are. We should understand how important our unique greatness and talents are. How can we use those talents to make this world a better place?

The world needs to hear each of our voices. We cannot speak up if we are hiding behind the uncertainty of who we are or the lies that society has told us.

This is **so** important.

The right way to self-promote is to think about it in the context of how it can help others. How will sharing my accomplishments help others? How does promoting my skills and abilities place me in a position to help someone else? You can also consider who is missing out by not hearing about what you can do. It is selfish to hide our talents under a bowl.

"You are the light of the world. A town built on a hill cannot be hidden. Neither do people light a lamp and put it under a bowl. Instead, they put it on its stand, and it gives light to everyone in the house." (**Matthew 5:14–15**)

What is the Scripture referring to here? What does it mean to hide your light under a bowl? It means concealing your talents and abilities for fear of appearing arrogant. Or you may be concealing things because of fear. Either way, the Scripture paints this act of perceived modesty as something somewhat negative.

Steps to take

1. Set your timer for five minutes (I am being generous). List twenty things that you love about yourself. When the time is up, how many things were you able to come up with?

2. If you were able to list twenty things in the allotted time, fantastic job! If not, why do you think that is?

3. Are you able to come up with twenty things if you do not have a time limit?

4. Take time to come up with the rest of the list without the timer. This is an important exercise to complete.

5. List five qualities that you think your friends would use to describe you. Ask ten people.

6. Compare your list to the qualities that these ten people give you. Are there any surprises? Are there qualities that you do not like but now realize? What about the great qualities that surprise you? What will you do with this information? How can you apply it to improve your future?

7. Let's do something like the exercises we did before. This time rather than focus on what you love about yourself, I would like you to focus on your accomplishments. List as many accomplishments as you can think of as far back as you can remember. There is no limit on how many accomplishments you write, but I want you to write at least ten.

8. Pick one accomplishment that you would like to share with the world. This accomplishment can be your story. Consider how you can help other people by sharing this accomplishment. What light can you shine to guide others?

Section 3:
E is for Engine

Chapter 9
Health and Well Being

You can't give what you don't have

I have four quadrants in which I place everything. They are:

1. Sleep

2. Prayer

3. Nutrition

4. Exercise

I achieve my greatest sense of balance when and only when I am doing well in all four quadrants, which is hardly ever. What does balance mean anyway?

Do you ever keep going until you feel like you have run out of steam?

Do you find yourself getting resentful because you never have the time to do the things that you want to do?

Do you wake up in the morning excited to face the day? Or does it take you time to adapt to the idea of facing a new day?

It is impossible to give what we do not have. Every engine needs maintenance, and you are an engine.

A few weeks ago, I found myself exhausted and spent. It was 5 p.m. on a Saturday evening. I had not accomplished much and still had a huge to-do list. I was so tired that I could barely keep my eyes open despite a looming mountain of work to still complete. My twins had been home all day, and I had promised them that we would go out in the evening. My husband was out of town and my twelve-year-old was at a friend's house for the evening.

This was the narrative I told myself that evening:

> *I feel like I am on the verge of a nervous breakdown. I have never had a nervous breakdown, but if I am asked to describe what I think it might feel like, I would describe how I am feeling right now.*
>
> *I have bitten off way more than I can chew, and there is no one to ask for help. I am*

supposed to be the one that has it all together. I am the one that other people run to when they are feeling overwhelmed. I always know what to say and I always have a word of encouragement that leaves them feeling like they can go on.

I host a podcast to celebrate Igbo women and Igbo culture. I have been hosting this podcast for nine months. It has been more work than I ever could have imagined with little reward or sign that it is worth it.

I am told to keep going and reminded that it is great that my podcast is targeted to such a niche audience. It takes up hours of my time to find guests to interview. Additionally, I have to schedule the guests, record the interview and edit the show. Finally, I need to publish to the host, send an email to my list, and post on social media.

That would be okay if it was the only thing, but it is not the only thing. I have a demanding job, and on top of it all, I am writing a book. I have never written a book before. I have no idea what I am doing. What are you thinking? Why are you doing all this? What are you trying to prove?

Have you experienced a similar situation? A situation where maybe all you wanted to do was give up?

So, this is what I told myself to get myself away from the verge of a complete meltdown:

> *Ugochi, the honest answer is "Nothing." You do not have to prove anything. You are enough whether you do any of this or none of it. You know that you have to try. You have to go to your grave spent, tapped out, having poured yourself out like water.*

> *Nothing less will do. So, you may sit here with a target goal of words to write for today. You may be tired, cranky, and discouraged. Yet, you know that you have to keep going. When all is said and done, the world needs to hear your story. You will not be complete if you do not pursue all that is stirring in your heart.*

Have you tried speaking to yourself in a similar manner when you feel discouraged? How helpful did you find it?

Despite our best efforts, some days are just hard. Remember that the great thing about a new day is that you can wipe the slate clean and try again. I love the quote "Aluta Continua." It means "the struggle continues." Always we begin again. Tomorrow is another day.

Remember though, it is not possible to give what you do not have. We should also be focused on our health and well-being.

God, in his infinite wisdom, created twenty-four hours in the day. It is important to rest. So, when you find yourself in a situation like this, the best thing you can do is to allow yourself an early night. It may also be a good idea to take a nap or go for a walk. That may be just what you need to tackle your challenge.

For me, an early bedtime helped in my moment of overwhelm. I did not take my twins out that evening. Instead, I did what I could and went to bed. I woke up the next day very refreshed. The twins and I went out to lunch the next day after church, which was just as enjoyable as the evening plans. My decision to rest had helped me to keep going and thrive.

Listen to your internal cues. You need to keep your engine running and maintained to achieve your goals.

In my case, I need to make sure I get to sleep. I also need to make sure that prayer is a focus. I need to find time to exercise, and I need to make sure that I eat well. The reason for this is that it is otherwise impossible to sustain such a busy pace of life. Something will have to give, and I do not want it to be me.

It's important to define your quadrants.

Based on my experience and my friends and colleagues' experience, here are the other things that could fill the quadrants:

- Dance

- Painting and art

- Writing

- Meditation

- Spending time with friends

This is not an exhaustive list, but it might spark some inspiration for you.

Self-care

We may encourage ourselves or be motivated to achieve our goals, but we also need listen to our body, soul, and spirit. If we do not listen to internal cues, we can drive ourselves into the ground.

This is an area in which I struggle because I have such a strong desire to reach my goals. I am sure you do too, otherwise you would not be reading this book.

It is important to recognize the early signs of burnout and to respond. Burnout is a long process to recover from and we do not want to allow ourselves to reach that point.

What are some of the signs that we need to scale back to avoid early burnout?

> *Burnout, defined as a state of physical, emotional and mental exhaustion, typically occurs as a result of working with people over long periods of time in situations that are emotionally demanding.*[2]

It is important to note that burnout does not happen overnight. It is often a slow process that we need to address before it gets to the point of burnout.

The best way to combat the risk of burnout is through self-care.

Self-care, in my view, is taking time out to care for yourself. We cannot give what we do not have. It is important for us to take breaks and spend time enjoying what it is that fuels us and energizes us.

Self-care includes rest, relaxation, proper nutrition, sleep, and spending time with loved ones. Those are

---

[2] Pines, Ayala and Aronson, Elliot. (1983). Combatting Burnout. *ScienceDirect Children and Youth Services Review*, 5(3), 263-275.

obvious methods of self-care. Yet, activities considered to be self-care are unique to each individual.

Self-care takes discipline. As driven, high achievers it is actually difficult to pause and step away. As Mothers, there is always so much on our plate, but we need to recharge for the long haul. Treat self-care as a marathon, not a sprint.

As an ex-marathon runner, I know all too well the pacing of the long, slow distance. If I set out in the first mile at a pace that is too fast, I am exhausted by the time I get to the ninth mile. I will likely be unable to complete the distance. Or I will end up walking the rest of the way and not finish within the race allowed time. Trust me—I have had occasions where I have come close to not receiving a medal.

The Marine Corps Marathon in Washington DC coined the term "beating the bridge." The bridge is at mile twenty of the 26.2-mile race. You had to get to that bridge within a certain time, or you would not be able to complete the race. This is because the race officials had to reopen the roads. Once you got to the bridge within the required time, you are said to have "beat the bridge."

For slow runners like me, it was important to know how to pace myself. This was to ensure I could run fast enough to beat the bridge. It was a balance between not starting out at too quick of a pace or not getting to the bridge at all.

Settle in because the marathon is very much like life itself. Be patient, and pace yourself. The race is not completed in the first ten miles.

Ecclesiastes 9:11 tells us, "**The race is not to the swift**, or the battle to the strong..."

This means that it is not the fastest person in a race nor is it the strongest person in a battle that is the most successful. Rather, it is the person that consistently works towards their goal that achieves it.

Find an outlet

Everyone needs something that they can do to get away from it all and get that release from the pressures of daily life.

What is that one thing that you love to do that helps you relax? Is it a massage, a long run, or a spin class? Maybe it's meeting up with friends or spending some quality time alone.

We all need activities in which we can take part to help us to blow off steam. Identifying those activities can help us avoid burnout. By doing them, Mothers are taking care of themselves so they can tackle all of the other things on their plate.

Steps to take

1. Schedule time on your calendar this week for self-care. Take some time to do something that will help to recharge your batteries.

2. Schedule time on your calendar once a month to recharge. Plan this time with family and engage their help if, for example, you need someone to watch the children.

Chapter 10
Sleep

Sleep

A big question for all Mothers is "How do I get enough sleep?" I'll make recommendations on ways to get a better night's sleep below. Yet, all this great advice could leave you rolling your eyes if you have to get up three times a night to feed a crying baby. You may also be kept up at night worrying about a deadline and how you are expected to juggle it all. But sleep still needs to be a priority.

Your child

If you have young children, it is important for them to sleep well so you can get good sleep too.

I have listed ways to help your children sleep better at night. Of course, we know as Mothers that even the most seemingly helpful routine or suggestion does not come with a 100% guarantee to work all of the time. But, I have made this journey, and I can attest that these simple tips do help even if only a little.

Most children and teenagers do not get enough sleep. It is a struggle, particularly for teenagers (like mine) who have the demands of rigorous schoolwork. That, coupled with extracurricular activities, means that they often go to bed late.

Not all the tips will apply at each stage of a child's life to the same degree. But I believe that the tips below will help children of all ages, even teenagers.

1. Have your child go to bed at the same time each night.

2. Do not allow televisions or electronic devices in the room with your child at night.

3. Have your child use an alarm clock to prevent them from using the alarm on their phone.

4. Leave two or three hours between the last meal of the day and bedtime.

5. Use a corridor light or night light so your child is not in complete darkness. This may help some children to feel less scared and fall asleep easier.

6. Read a bedtime story. I would try to make up a story on the spot for my youngest son, but that did not always work out so well. I chuckle as I think about this because my son was a tough listener. He would often poke holes in my story. Sometimes my stories would be a hit, other times not so much. Still, he would always insist that I read him a story or make one up. It did not matter whether or not my story was up to a certain standard.

7. Get your child in the habit of saying a quick prayer during their bedtime routine. A routine creates a signal for bed.

8. Play music softly in your child's room. This helped one of my sons, but my daughter didn't like it.

Remember each child is different. If you establish a routine that utilizes a combination of these approaches, that will help everyone in the end. It may take some experimentation, but it's worth the effort to discover what works for you and your child.

You

I want you to go to bed early. I want you to sleep well and wake up refreshed.

I need to sleep. I have always prioritized sleep and arranged my schedule to revolve around a good night's sleep.

For me, a good night's sleep is eight hours. I can work with seven hours of sleep, but with any amount of sleep less than that, I am unable to run on all cylinders.

A lack of sleep causes me to overeat, and I start to crave processed carbohydrates and sugar. I am less able to function, and I overreact to the smallest provocation.

If I have a week with concurrent nights of reduced sleep, I start to suffer from back pain.

I have conditioned myself to go to bed early and wake up early.

I aim to be in bed by 9:30 p.m., and I wake up at 5 a.m. This is the ideal scenario for me.

Hal Elrod, author of the *Miracle Morning*, writes the following:

> "How you wake up each day and your morning routine dramatically affects your levels of success in every single area of your life."[3]

As Hal mentions, if you get a good night's rest, you can awake with the energy to fulfill your morning routine and set yourself up for a successful day.

There are many ways to make sleep more of a priority. Below are some suggestions.

1. Do not use your phone as an alarm.

2. Turn the lights off to tell your body it is time to sleep.

3. Play soft music. This may be distracting, so it does not work for everyone.

4. Do not do work in bed.

5. Do not drink caffeine after 2 p.m. I find that drinking a caffeinated beverage after 2 p.m. affects my sleep. I heard somewhere that you

---

[3] Elrod, Hal. (2012). *The Miracle Morning: The Not-so-obvious Secret Guaranteed to Transform Your Life Before 8AM*. Hal Elrod International, Inc.

should stop drinking caffeine for about twelve hours before you go to bed. So, if you plan to be in bed by 10 p.m., you should pause drinking any caffeinated drinks after 10 a.m. That's a long time for anyone to go sans caffeine. Maybe five to six hours before bed could work for you.

6. Try to exercise in the morning. It is better to exercise in the evening than not at all if that is the only time that you can fit it in. But I find that when I work out in the evening, it is harder for me to go to sleep.

7. Try to organize your agenda for the next day before you go to sleep. This is so you do not lie in bed thinking about all the things that you have to do the next day.

Arianna Huffington, author of *The Sleep Revolution*[4], shares her own tips for getting a good night's sleep:

1. She turns off all her devices thirty minutes before bedtime.

2. She takes a hot bath.

3. She wears pajamas instead of what she used to wear to bed, which was gym clothes.

---

[4] Huffington, Arianna. (2017). *The Sleep Revolution: Transforming Your Life, One Night at a Time*. New York: Harmony Books.

4. She only reads physical books that "have nothing to do with work" when she's under the covers. These tend to be poetry, philosophy, and fiction books.

5. She takes the time to write down three things she's thankful for that day, giving the day a closing scene.

In the following section, I conclude this chapter by having you write in your journal. The goal is to get you to be intentional about a good night's sleep and write down specific things that you can do to achieve that, thus making you more productive during the day.

Steps to take

1. List three things that you will put into action to get a better night's sleep.

2. Try to go to bed early tonight and wake up earlier tomorrow. Make a note of how you feel.

3. Repeat that routine for three nights in a row. Make a note of how you feel. Do you feel any different than you did before? Write this down. You may not feel any different and that is fine.

However, you may find that you are more productive. If you do not feel any different, and you do not notice any change in effectiveness, find a routine that works for you. Everyone will have unique needs.

Chapter 11
Weight

As a Mother struggling to get through the day, your abs may be the last thing on your mind. You are probably also worried about your finances, marriage, work, or just making it through the day. Sometimes taking a shower is the greatest achievement of your day.

I always felt overwhelmed by the photos of the Moms with flat abs carrying a baby and a toddler.

I've learned that success is dependent on my definition, not anyone else's. No one else gets to define how much I should weigh, or what an ideal weight should be.

The scale

The scale, the dreaded scale.

Do you want to know how I got over the fear of standing on the scale? Well, it is simple...I stood on the scale.

Yup, that is it. I stood on the scale. Then I stood on the scale the next day and the day after that.

You see, doing something that you are afraid of makes you fear it less. It is that simple.

So regardless of the number, stand on the scale. Embrace the number that you see. Take a deep breath. Besides, no one else needs to know the number that you see on the scale unless you decide to share it.

I found out the hard way that I can't control what I do not measure. But it is important to say that the scale does not have to be your measure of success. There are so many ways to determine your success, and I reiterate that it depends on what you choose to measure.

There are many non-scale victories that I have celebrated in my journey. Those have been sweeter than the number on the scale.

Managing my weight has been a challenging journey. But a specific number was not my destination. I am learning (slowly) that I rock regardless of the number on the scale. I have been a few sizes, and I am beautiful at every size.

When I was pregnant with my twins, I gained 100 pounds. I will never forget the day I sat in the OB/GYN's office and my weight had crossed the 200-pound mark.

I sat in her office and cried. I was pregnant with twins, yes, but at that moment, I felt like I had lost all control. It is funny because I gained another fifty pounds after that day.

My doctor sent me to a nutritionist who told me that I had a "big" body, much bigger than hers. So, my portion sizes would not be the same as what she would eat. What a way to make me feel better, sister. On a separate note, why are some women like this? Why do we put other people down to feel better about ourselves?

On a separate note, I found the definition of charisma. That situation reminded me that a charismatic person makes other people feel good about themselves. I want to be charismatic. Don't you too?

Back to weight...

On the day of my twins' birth, I stood on the scale at 248 pounds. It turns out I had preeclampsia and was retaining a ton of water. This was the main reason for a lot of the weight gain. Still after all the water weight was gone, I had thirty pounds to lose. I could not blame that on water weight.

It took me almost a year to lose sixteen pounds, and the other fourteen pounds would not budge. That weight came off in time and with patience.

Mothers, we have all been there. Our bodies have birthed life. How amazing are we? The struggle with weight is real, but we are all in this together.

Four years later, when I had my youngest child, I gained about fifty-five pounds. The morning of his birth (this time it was a single pregnancy), I weighed 204 pounds.

The weight came off a little easier that time, but I confess that I did work a lot harder to get it off.

I joined Weight Watchers, and I worked out five days each week for an hour, doing cardio to burn calories.

I remember one weight management issue vividly. I had returned from vacation and I had not weighed myself in months. I knew that I had gained a few pounds, but I did not want to know how bad it was.

I received a rude awakening when I visited the doctor for my annual checkup. The nurse made me stand on the scale, and I noticed that she kept sliding the bar to the right. She kept going and going. I could feel the sense of dread continue to rise.

Then she announced (a little too loudly, if you ask me), "You have gained quite a bit of weight." I look down at the scale. I had gained fifteen pounds. That may not seem like a lot of weight, but as you age, it is harder to maintain the same weight range as when you are younger.

So, I enlisted the help of my friend, Kwavi, who is a midlife life coach and a weight coach. Kwavi put me to work. She made me return to my habit of weighing myself daily. She also had me keep a food journal and write down everything that passed through my lips. This included gum and water.

It took months of hard work, but I was finally able to lose weight.

The unfortunate thing about weight loss is that the journey is never-ending. You can't achieve a goal weight and be done. It is another task to maintain the weight loss. This can be as difficult as losing the weight in the first place.

I have accepted that maintaining weight is an ongoing journey without a destination. I also have accepted that there will be times when I am doing well and other times when I don't do so well. At the end of the day, consistency is the name of the game.

Weight management is important to my well-being. I now have a healthy weight range goal for my height and body frame. I work hard to stay within that range, but I am also realistic. It is a journey after all.

We are all in this together for the long haul. Don't focus on the number on the scale. Focus on your health.

Steps to take

Use your journal to make notes for yourself about your weight goals and management.

1. Take an honest stock of whether you are within a healthy weight range. Remember that this is about your overall health. Make sure that your engine (that's you) is in prime condition.

2. Be realistic and understand that weight management is a journey with no destination. Be proud and embrace yourself wherever you are on the journey. No one else gets to define what you should weigh or what size is acceptable. You are on this journey toward good health to enable you to be the best Mother that you can be.

3. Try cutting down on alcohol.

4. Drink more water. I aim to drink about six eight-ounce glasses a day. Of course, this does not always happen, but I try because it does help.

5. Watch what you eat. Cutting out or cutting down on dairy, sugar, and wheat have made a big difference in my weight loss journey (more details coming up).

6. If you are struggling to manage weight on your own, I have found that the best way to solve this is to enlist an accountability partner. My close friend Ada and I text each other after each workout. We committed to each other that we would work out at least four times a week. We often create challenges together. She might say "Ugochi, let's not eat sugar for the next three weeks." This is a fun way to engage in something together. She is a great accountability partner.

In the next chapter, we look beyond the number on the scale as we discuss nutrition and exercise. We'll talk about the important role that both play in our health and well-being.

Chapter 12
Nutrition and Exercise

In this chapter, we talk about the role nutrition and exercise have in our lives. Please remember that I am sharing my journey and the things that have worked for me. I am in no way a nutritionist or fitness expert. My goal is not to tell you what you should be doing. Rather I share my approach, even if it is imperfect. My hope is that it will encourage you along your journey.

Nutrition

There are four categories of items that I consume that have a significant impact on the way that I feel. It has taken me years to realize the effect these four categories have on my health. But when I recognized their impact on my ability to function, I knew something had to change.

- Wheat

- Dairy

- Sugar

- Alcohol

In some way shape or form, my body does not like anything in the four categories listed above.

If I eat wheat more than once a week, my body starts to ache, and I experience intense fatigue that I find hard to describe. I also start to develop swollen glands around my neck.

When I eat a lot of dairy products, my skin starts to break out in a rash and spots.

When I eat a lot of sugar, I get bad headaches and feel nauseated.

Does this mean that I don't eat food from these categories, ever? No, I like to be able to enjoy what I eat. I just eat from these categories sparingly because I am aware of the effect on my system.

How did I discover my intolerance for these food categories? It happened over time and through the use of experimentation. I had to focus on listening to my body. Through trial and error, I started to notice these symptoms. I would ask myself why I felt so fatigued and achy. I started to question what I had eaten over the last several days.

One way to assess your potential intolerances is to try eliminating certain food categories completely from your diet for one week. Note how you feel.

The next week, reintroduce one food category and note how you feel. Wait a couple of days before you reintroduce the second food category. This will give you time to assess the impact the first food category has on your system.

Repeat this for the third food category and wait a couple of days. Finally, reintroduce the fourth food category.

Be sure to log everything that you eat. Take notes throughout the process regarding how you feel. Some of the changes may be subtle. But by the end of this experiment, you will have a clearer picture of the effect these foods have on your system.

In some cases, total elimination may be necessary. In other cases, cutting down on the quantity of these foods you consume will be fine. Everybody is different, and you know what works for you.

I had to learn to view food as fuel and medicine. I try to eat a diet with limited to no processed foods. I find that I am better able to function (with less brain fog) if I am eating as healthy as I can. I also try to drink water for my beverage of choice. But if I crave a cookie, I will have one cookie. A little indulgence can be a good thing.

I do not drink any alcohol mainly because I do not like the way it tastes. Yet, some people enjoy alcohol and find that it can be healthy in moderation (like red wine, for example).

Good nutrition limits the likelihood of major illnesses and helps us Mothers stay healthy.

I do believe that nutrition is helpful along your journey. Some days we do well, and on other days, we could do better. The slate is clean the next day as long as we resolve to do better. Over time, each day's efforts toward our commitment to maintain healthy nutrition habits will yield positive results.

Exercise

Exercise is a very important part of a healthy lifestyle. The American Medical Association recommends twenty minutes of exercise at least three times a week.

That is a great starting point, but similar to nutrition, exercise is a case of "different strokes for different folks."

Everyone needs to move. Our bodies were not created to be sedentary. Exercise is a gift that I give my body. I appreciate the fact that I have the health and strength to move.

I have friends who do gentle yoga stretches as part of an exercise regime. Other friends prefer the brutal boot camps at 5 a.m. Some people may like to swim laps or take a walk, while others work out to the point of exhaustion.

Exercise is not one-size-fits-all, so it is important to find the type of exercise that you enjoy.

That does not mean that because I enjoy a certain activity that I want do it four to six times a week. There will be mornings (most mornings) that you or I will not want to get out of bed. This is where motivation and discipline have to kick in.

Despite how much I haven't wanted to exercise, I have never regretted doing a workout. Have you?

I used to love being outside running and walking. I loved setting the goal of running races. These days, I prefer more toning and Pilates–type exercise, which is just as challenging for me.

At the end of the day, the most important thing is to find an exercise that you enjoy and stick to it.

Steps to take

1. Decide what exercise you enjoy enough to take part in four to six times a week.

2. Make a commitment to yourself to start regular exercise. Start slowly and build up to four to six times a week.

3. Never depend on how you feel as an indicator of whether you should exercise. Take the emotion out of it, just like you do while washing your hair or brushing your teeth.

4. Stick with this for four weeks. At the end of four weeks, note how you feel.

5. Switch up your exercise. Exercising regularly is a lifestyle and should be fun.

In the next section, we focus on relationships. Knowing about ourselves and analyzing our connections are both critical to maintaining quality relationships.

Section 4:
R is for Relationships

Chapter 13
The Source of It All

This book would not be authentic if I did not bring the whole of me into the picture.

The core of who I am has roots in my strong faith in God. I will explain why this faith is so important to me and how it has affected my life and made me who I am today. I'll also discuss relationships and the people that make it possible for us to be successful in life. We cannot survive or succeed on our own. We need other people to help us along the way, and in the same way that we provide help to others.

What has carried me through all the seasons of my life, even some seasons that have been incredibly difficult?

My faith in God. That has been the one thing that has carried me through everything. That Faith has seen me through the good and the bad.

To me, God is the source of everything that I am. I was made in His image, and He is my source.

Without Him, there is no me. Everything that I am or could ever hope to be is in Him.

He is my Creator, my Master, and my Help in troubled times.

My faith grounds me and helps me to focus on my path.

When I reflect on who my source is, I picture a flowing river that never runs dry.

I plug into Him for strength, for wisdom, for peace, for confidence, for grace, and for mercy.

My faith gives me the strength to face every day.

Psalm 18:32 says, "It is God who arms me with strength and keeps my way secure."

This is my mantra, and I quote this verse of Scripture to myself often. I reflect on this verse of Scripture before any hard or challenging tasks.

A relationship with God through prayer and meditation

Prayer is talking to God.

I pray all the time—having children makes you do that. I prayed when they had a cold or a cough as babies, I prayed when they were asleep, and I prayed when they were at school. I prayed when they were happy and when they were sad.

Today, I pray when they have a great day at school. I also pray when they have problems with friendships. I pray now that they are learning to drive. I pray when they are out of the house.

It is interesting because I still pray all the time, but my prayers are different depending on the situation. Prayer shows a complete reliance on God.

The best time for me to pray is early, although prayer can be done at any time. For me, prayer in the early hours sets me up for the day.

I pray at work. I pray in the car at 4:30 a.m., when I am driving back from dropping my daughter at the boathouse for early morning crew practice.

The best way to engage in prayer is to talk to God as if He is right next to you.

Learning to pray is one of the most important things we can do in our lives.

As a Mother, prayer plays a huge part in my life. I draw a lot of strength and courage from prayer, which helps me to deal with the challenges of parenting three children. I can talk to God about anything that arises, and then I'm better able to handle any issues.

Prayer is something most people understand the importance of. But few feel they have a successful prayer life. You can define a prayer routine that is meaningful and helpful to you.

Ask, Seek, Knock

When we come before God to pray, it is helpful to know that He hears us. He is our heavenly Father. Prayer is talking to your Father in heaven. If I wanted something from my Dad I would go to him and ask.

For me to receive what I wanted, I had to ask for it. Prayer is also a conversation. It is a way to seek a stronger relationship with God. I also believe that prayer is a key to unlocking a full life. I use the following verses of Scripture to illustrate the power of prayer.

> *"Ask and it will be given to you; seek and you will find; knock and the door will be opened to you. For everyone who asks receives; the one who seeks finds; and to the one who knocks, the door will be opened.*
>
> *Which of you, if your son asks for bread, will give him a stone? Or if he asks for a fish, will give him a snake? If you, then, though you are evil, know how to give good gifts to your children, how much more will your Father in heaven give good gifts to those who ask him!"*
>
> **(Matthew 7:7–11)**

Jesus placed a huge priority on prayer. He prayed:

- **early.** Very early in the morning, while it was still dark, Jesus got up, left the house, and went off to a solitary place, where he prayed (**Mark 1:35**).

- **late.** One of those days Jesus went out to a mountainside to pray, and he spent the night praying to God (**Luke 6:12**).

- **often.** But Jesus often withdrew to lonely places and prayed (**Luke 5:16**).

- **before critical events in his life.** This is demonstrated through **John 17**.

The Bible is called the Word of God. It is a living, breathing, dynamic document of God's heart. It is the spoken word of God put on paper for us to live by. It has been a guide for me. For every situation in life, there is a verse of Scripture that applies. It does not matter how unique that particular situation may be.

The quiet time before anyone is awake is a special time for me to gather my thoughts and focus on what is important. I can quiet my mind and reflect. I will often pick a verse of Scripture and meditate on that.

Prayer is the biggest tool through which I will fulfill my life's purpose. During my prayer time, I draw strength, encouragement, and guidance for each day.

Steps to take

1. Think about ways that you can partner with God to fulfill your purpose. Spend time in prayer seeking His will for your life. Resolve to submit your life into His hands.

2. What are some practical ways that you can set aside time to pray every day?

In the next chapter, we discuss the family and our place within it. I was born into the family that I was for a reason. I married into the family that I did for a reason. The people who are part of my family are a key part of my destiny and have helped to shape who I have become.

Chapter 14
Family

It is interesting that the Bible says in **Psalm 68:6** that God sets the lonely in families. The family unit has a specific purpose for our lives. The purpose is bigger than having people to love, people to annoy us, or people to argue with over Thanksgiving dinner.

A family is a group of people that God has placed in our lives to cheer us on and provide support.

Family is so important to us Mothers. We need people to step in and help out at a moment's notice. I understand that not all family members are able or willing to help out when needed. But for the most part, we will have family members who will drop everything and rush to our side when we need help.

I struggled a lot as a young Mother because I did not have any of my family members in the same location. My Mother, two brothers, and my younger sister all live in the U.K. I have three older sisters who live in Nigeria, so I am the only member of the family in the U.S.

My Mother did come and spend a few weeks with me when I had my babies. But it was not the same as having her close when I wanted someone to talk to over coffee. My younger sister is an easy phone call away, so at least we can spend many hours on the phone when needed.

Still, my husband has a large family, and I have grown close to those family members. I am particularly close to his three beautiful sisters who I now consider to be my sisters. We have spent many family gatherings together laughing and chatting. I love them very much.

Family members could be spouses, significant others, parents, siblings, aunts, uncles, sisters-in-law, brothers-in-law, cousins, or cousins of cousins. Having a good relationship with family members is very important to me even if I do not see them every day.

Yet, the nuclear family is the most important unit for us as Mothers, and for our children. It is the way that they learn to interact with the world around them. The way that we treat each other within the family is critical. It will teach our children how to treat other people outside of the home.

Family members make great babysitters as I am sure you can attest to. As you work toward accomplishing your goals, family members are indispensable. They are great resources for helping to pick up the slack. This is important as you focus on the tasks that will get you to your goal.

Steps to take

The purpose of the following steps is to analyze our current family relationships. There may be members of the family from whom you have drifted. Spend some time answering the following questions in your journal.

1. Take a few moments to journal a response to the following questions: Who in your family do you need to mend a relationship with? How can you go about doing that?

2. Now take some time to answer these questions: What are some things that you can do to improve family relationships? How can you become a more supportive member of your family?

In the next chapter, I talk about the tribe. This is something about which I am passionate.

My goal is to build a tribe of F.I.E.R.C.E Mothers. And you are now a part of that tribe by reading this book. We are Mothers who journey through life together and celebrate each other along the way.

Chapter 15
Like Minds

"Walk with the wise and become wise, for a companion of fools suffers harm." (**Proverbs 13:20**)

A tribe is so important to our well-being as humans. In my mind, a tribe is a group of people with whom you can identify. You can walk among your tribe and feel like you are at home. This group of people understands you and accepts you as you are. In today's world, your tribe could be physical or virtual.

Your tribe is your clan, your community, your kind of people. It's not limited by size or even how well you know its members.

For example, with this book, we have created a tribe of F.I.E.R.C.E Mothers. This tribe has many members who we may never meet. But we have a connection with one other as we travel the same journey.

You can belong to different tribes, some large and some small, as I will explain in this chapter. Regardless, everyone needs at least one tribe.

Ride or Die

The Urban Dictionary explains the phrase "Ride or Die"[5] as follows:

> Ride or Die was originally a biker term meaning if you couldn't ride you'd rather die. It has now changed to mean anyone (wife, boyfriend, best friend), that you will "ride" ANY problems out with them or "die" trying. The "ride" doesn't always have to be a negative either. Obviously if you're this close to someone you want them to enjoy the "ride" (life and all it has to offer with them as well).

You are much stronger than you think. But sometimes your strength is not enough to reach the goals that you are trying to meet.

This is why you need to surround yourself with people who encourage you. These are people that have a similar

[5] Urban Dictionary. (2015). "Ride or Die." Retrieved from https://www.urbandictionary.com/define.php?term=Ride%20or%20Die.

desire to achieve their purpose and destiny. They are your tribe.

Nothing great has been achieved in isolation. You can feel like you are more efficient if you do things by yourself, and to some degree, this can be true. But, this is a shortsighted way to look at things.

There is an African proverb that says "if you want to go fast, go alone, but if you want to go far, go together."

There are different types of friends. Some are friends that you may call on for a specific occasion. You may have friends that you call when you want to go shoe shopping, or need help styling an outfit. Other friends may be helpful as accountability partners. You may have specific friends that you would call at 2 a.m. during a crisis. They are all still friends but each plays a unique role.

Not everyone will be in your inner circle, but the need for human connection is very real. I love meeting new people and making new connections.

When I reflect on the role of friendships and people that I keep close, I picture the life of Jesus.

Jesus had three people who were closest to him—Peter, James, and John. Then He had the twelve disciples who were also part of the inner circle. And He had fifty apostles who were instructed to go out into the world and preach the gospel. Those fifty apostles were told to shake the dust off their feet at the doorstep of anyone that did not welcome them in.

These fifty apostles came back rejoicing to the Lord. They told Him about all of the signs and wonders that they had experienced.

We would say that all these people were part of Jesus' tribe. Yet, even within his tribe, he had some people that were closer to him than others.

You do not want to be the smartest in the room all the time. You also shouldn't be the person everyone looks up to. You should always be around a tribe that makes you want to leave your comfort zone. The members of your tribe want you to continue getting and doing better. The people around you should encourage you to bring out your "A game".

On the flip side, being outside of your comfort zone does not have to be the norm. It's impossible to strike a balance if you are only on the receiving end and always looking up to others. I think it's healthy to balance the time by contributing to your tribe. You can contribute by imparting wisdom to others and help them.

The Bible says that to whom much is given, much is expected.

So, when considering your tribe, know that's sometimes you are the one dishing out the wisdom, sometimes you are receiving the wisdom. Iron sharpens Iron.

In addition to my younger sister, I have a small circle of people in my life who are my tribe. I know that whenever there is a crisis or an emergency, I can call or text them and they will spring into action. I do not take this for granted, especially in a world where we have hundreds or even thousands of "friends" through social media.

I also have a small Bible study group that I belong to. This is a group of dear friends, and I have been part of this group for close to ten years. We only meet about once a quarter, but we have been through so much together. Some of the events we've faced together include:

- the death of loved ones

- pregnancy concerns

- a child's cancer diagnosis

- anxiety over a decision

- career challenges

- starting businesses

Our tribe does life together.

It is so important to have that inner circle, your crew, your tribe. If you don't have one already, I hope you'll find joy in forming one.

Accountability groups

Like I said before, you cannot go it alone. Trust me, this was a hard fact for me to accept because by nature I am an extreme introvert. The perfect day for me is a day of solitude, a day when I can pray, sleep, read, work out, all without interacting with anyone.

But, I am also a people person. It sounds like a big contradiction, but it is true. I love people. I hate to see people in pain. My struggle is accepting that I cannot help everyone.

I understand if you feel like it is easier, more efficient, or even better to do things on your own. It is not true. The saying that no (wo)man is an island is so true. You need other people to arrive at your destination. It's the way the universe works.

So, with that knowledge, what do you do if you feel isolated, or if you do not feel you have a connection to people of "like minds"? Create or join a group of like-minded individuals.

I can hear you now. You are probably thinking, "Ugochi, seriously? Create a small group on top of everything else that I have to do? Do you know how much I have on my plate? This is one more thing I have to organize."

I understand. If you are able, have an accountability group that meets once every three months. Or if you are overwhelmed with life, create a virtual meet up.

You could even start by using the WhatsApp messenger app and create your group. It allows for instant connection despite time apart. Keep the group small in the beginning. My bible group started as five people, and we have discussed adding more people. But we love that we are so close, and we crave each other's presence after a few months. It's okay to stay small with a group of people that you know well, that you trust, and that you love.

In your group, whether in-person or virtual, challenge each other. Bring ideas, pose questions, and seek advice. You don't have to share deep personal secrets or problems, unless of course, you want to. The connection may be as simple as bouncing ideas off each other about a job interview or starting a small business. It could even be as simple as accountability for an exercise or diet program.

That small group helps with accountability to accomplish your goals. You need someone that you can share results with. You need someone to check in to see whether you did what you said you were going to do.

You also need a place where you can share your struggles. Maybe you've made several goals but struggle to stay motivated. By sharing that within your accountability group, someone could say something that gives you an "aha" moment. Or the group could just listen to you. But when things go well, you also need a place to share your victories and be celebrated.

Having accountability makes all the difference. Join a group, or reach out to two or three people with a similar drive and purpose. They may be stuck in a rut too. Starting an accountability group will help us Mothers to motivate and support each other.

Steps to take

1. Take a moment to list three to five people who you know that you could call at 2 a.m., and they would spring into action. Or maybe you have people who will instinctively show up at your door to help without you asking them to come.

2. Think about how many people would put you in that category. Why do you think they would count you as part of their "Ride or Die" tribe?

In the next section, we talk about a critical area of our lives—our finances. In this section, I will help you to understand how you are the Chief Financial Officer, or CFO, of your life. You are the CFO of your everyday life as well as your financial life. We will start by unpacking our relationships with money and how we view wealth.

C is for Chief Financial Officer

Chapter 16
Relationships with Money

When I was seventeen years old, I left Nigeria to return to London where I was born. My parents had sent my brother and me to the U.K. for the equivalent of our junior and senior years in high school. The intention was to prepare us to go to college in the U.K. Two years later, my Mother joined my brother and me in London. She brought my younger brother and sister too.

So, at that point, all my Mother's children were in the U.K. My Father had stayed back in Nigeria with his work. He held the huge financial burden of paying our school tuition and other living expenses. My Mother also started work to help pay the bills and support the family.

But business did not go so well for my Father, and he became unable to pay tuition. At that time, my younger brother and sister were both in a private boarding school. I was in my freshman year in university.

My brother and sister had to withdraw from boarding school. They completed high school in a public school, which was tuition free.

I had to withdraw from university and spent the rest of the year working as a receptionist in an office of a patisserie. My small income only helped a bit with household expenses like groceries.

When all of this happened, I was only nineteen years old. I decided back then that I would always aim to have control over my own financial affairs.

My relationship with money, and my need to be in control of my own finances may be rooted in pain and disappointment. Yet, that disappointment has prompted me to work super hard. Being independent helps you to avoid resentment that you may otherwise experience. This resentment could arise when you trust someone else for your financial well-being.

I listened to the podcast called "How to Get Rich" by Naval Ravikant.[6] The podcast has a series of episodes with each one focusing on a different topic within wealth creation. Ravikant defines wealth as freedom, and I agree with that.

Wealth has nothing to do with what size house you live in or what expensive brands you wear. It doesn't have anything to do with the cars that you drive. None of that has to do with wealth. Instead, wealth is a tool that gives you the freedom to fulfill your goals and purpose.

---

[6] Ravikant, Naval. (2019, June 3). **How to Get Rich – Every Episode** [Audio **podcast**].

From my personal perspective, wealth means having enough to live on and enough to help the less fortunate. For me, it is that simple. I have driven the same car for thirteen years and will drive it till it dies.

In my mind, having a positive relationship with money is critical. After all, money is a tool that we are to use with wisdom. The degree to which I steward the financial resources that I have will determine how wealthy I am. I measure using my own definition of wealth.

Becoming wealthy and staying wealthy is a goal of mine, for which I am unapologetic.

Resources in the right hands will change the world, and I want to be someone with the right hands. As I discussed earlier, I wanted to be in control of financial decisions from a young age. Stewarding finances the right way helps me stay in control of my financial health.

Steps to take

1. In your journal, define wealth on your own terms. What does it mean to you to be wealthy?

2. What relationship do you have with money? Are you frugal or more extravagant?

3. Do you believe that your relationship with money stems from personal experience? Was that experience positive or negative?

4. How do you think that you need to change your relationship with money to be able to achieve wealth on your terms?

5. Do you believe that you will need to earn more money to be wealthy, using your definition of wealth? Or do you need to save more of what you earn?

In the next chapter, we discuss one of the simplest ways to take control of your financial life—creating a budget. We will define what exactly a budget is and why it is so important. Then you'll get to work creating a budget that works for you.

Chapter 17
Tracking Expenses

The Cambridge dictionary defines budget as an action "to plan to spend money for a particular purpose."

In my mind, a high-level budget is an effective way to track spending and make sure that you live within your means. You cannot track what you do not measure, and we tend to spend more when we don't track our spending.

Personal budgeting may not seem like fun. But it does help to save for the fun things in life without relying on a credit card to fund them.

Budgeting is not about how much we make even though we could all make more money. It is more about how much of what you earn that you are able to keep.

My goal is not for you to become a certified accountant or to make life miserable. I have heard individuals compare budgeting to dieting, neither of which work. Instead, I would like to walk you through (at a very high level) what works for me.

You may already have your own system, and if that is the case, please stick with what works for you.

You do not have to use my method if for some reason you prefer a deeper level of detail. Or you may prefer a different method to track your expenses. But I have two main tabs in my Excel spreadsheet that I use to track expenses, and they are: Monthly tracking and Daily expenditures.

Monthly tracking

I have created this sample budget below to show you how I track my monthly expenses.

The first tab of my Excel spreadsheet is **Monthly tracking**. To make your own monthly tracking, start by determining how much you need to support your household. You will do this by listing out all of your monthly expenses. Start by listing the highest expense and continue to the lowest expense.

So, your list may look something like this sample table.

Item	Amount
Mortgage	$1500
Groceries	$500
Electricity	$250
Car payment	$200
Cable	$150
Gas	$100
Car maintenance	$80
Gym	$60
Savings	$50
Manicure	$20

Figure 1: Monthly Expense Tracking

You will notice in the above example that I have two lines highlighted in green. I highlighted these two items because they are not expenses.

- The car maintenance is more of a buffer, or a pre-planned expense. I divide a certain amount of my income toward this so when the expense occurs, I have money set aside to cover it. This means I do not have to resort to using my credit card or delaying payments on other bills.

- The savings is for the short-term. It is like the car maintenance example. Others may call this an emergency fund. The funds can cover any unforeseen expenses.

You may have other rows for big purchases, travel funds, or miscellaneous.

The practice of listing out my monthly expenses has reduced my need for a credit card. It has helped me to spend more wisely and stay within my means.

Daily expenditures

The second tab in the Excel spreadsheet is **Daily expenditures**. It logs every expenditure that I make on a daily basis. I do not log each cash expenditure, but I will log the amount that I withdraw from the bank.

On this tab, I use the following columns:

- the date

- the vendor (example: Safeway, Amazon, Apple, etc.)

- debits

- credits

- balance

I use the zero-based budget method, a term I first heard from Dave Ramsey the radio host. The zero-based budgeting method is a system of budgeting where every penny is accounted for.

For each budget cycle, you should end with a balance of zero.

Does this mean that you have to spend every penny in your bank account? No, it means that there is a placeholder for all expenses. In a zero-based budget, your income minus your expenses should equal zero.

The zero-based budget method is the best way for me to put my money to work. It makes me feel that every cent has a purpose.

I take the data from my **Monthly tracking** tab and insert that into my **Daily expenditures** tab.

Before you do this, determine how you get paid. Is it monthly, bi-monthly, or weekly? For simplicity, let's assume that you receive a paycheck once a month. Take a look at the following example to understand how each expense is accounted for on the daily expenditures.

Date	Transaction	Credit	Debit	Balance
04/30/19	Paycheck	3000.00		3000.00
05/01	Mortgage		1500.00	1500.00
05/01	Groceries		500.00	1000.00
05/01	Electricity		250.00	750.00
05/01	Car payment		200.00	550.00
05/01	Cable		150.00	400.00
05/01	Gas		100.00	300.00
05/01	Car maintenance		80.00	220.00
05/01	Gym		60.00	160.00
05/01	Savings		50.00	110.00
05/01	Manicure		20.00	90.00
05/01	Cash withdrawal		90.00	00.00

Figure 2: Daily Expense Tracking

Note that in the example above, I withdraw $90 in cash, which will last me until my next paycheck.

Of course, the numbers and specific transactions will be different for you. But, this illustration explains the very simple way of tracking what you spend.

Whatever system you use, find a budget that forces you to account for every penny that you spend. I have been doing this for fifteen years, and this simple act alone has transformed my financial life. I'm not claiming to be a financial advisor, but this system helps to keep me on track.

I would recommend following a financial health program. My husband and I decided to follow the program outlined in Dave Ramsey's book, *Total Money Makeover*[7]. We started to see the true value of living below our means.

By God's grace, I control my money, and money does not control me. This does mean that there are so many things that I would love to have but cannot afford. On paper, it may look like I am able to afford more, but viewing wealth as a tool, it would not be a wise use of that tool for other purposes. As a result, I cannot afford those luxuries.

---

[7] Ramsey, Dave. (2009). *The Total Money Makeover: A Proven Plan for Financial Fitness*. Nashville, TN: Thomas Nelson.

That is not to say I don't treat myself—far from it. But, I am careful with the way that I spend money. God has blessed me with an income. I am called to be a steward of the three beautiful children He has blessed me with. In the same way, I am called to be a steward of the income He has provided. I am in no way comparing my children to my income, but I am saying that I have a responsibility to use my income wisely and to raise my children the right way.

Steps to take

I would suggest writing things down in your journal for brainstorming and then try using Excel. You could also use Google Sheets if you do not have Microsoft suite on your device.

1. Create your own simple method for tracking your expenses. You can perform a Google search and see what free sample budgets exist. Pick one that suits your style the most. For a download sample of my simple budget, visit http://www.fiercemothers.com/resources.

2. I am eager to hear what budgeting tool you choose. You can reach me at ugochi@fiercemothers.com.

In the next chapter, we cover short-term savings. By short-term, I mean six months to one year of savings in the bank. We will start off by understanding why it is important to save. I will then discuss some tips and ways to save more money or spend less.

Chapter 18
Saving

I define saving as a method of putting away a certain amount of money that you do not need, so you can use it in the future.

What is the importance of saving? Why should we do it? These may seem like very simple questions. They are important to answer, though, because at the root is the question of motivation. What is the "why" of saving? This will help you to keep going when you are tempted to deviate from the plan. I am always being tempted. There is always a cute outfit or pair of shoes that I just have to own.

But the main reason for me to save is to avoid going into debt in the future. Without funds in my bank account, I would have to use a credit card. That is something I try to avoid.

Saving in the context of this book refers to a short-term saving process. I am not discussing investments or long-term savings. I am not a financial expert, but I have discovered some practices that work well for me.

Saving and the emergency fund

The best vehicle by which to save for the short term is the emergency fund.

What is an emergency fund?

This is a fund for expenses that you do not budget for. In his book, *The Total Money Makeover*, Ramsey has a structure to create an emergency fund.

Ramsey recommends starting with at least $1,000.

I would suggest working up to three to six months of expenses. Now, this is a huge challenge, especially with children. They keep growing, and fast. I have to replace shoes and buy new uniforms for school on a regular basis. My grocery bill is one of my largest monthly bills.

In spite of this, I've found ways to help us to spend less money and funnel the extra to a separate account for my emergency fund. I discuss some of these strategies in the steps to take section. Remember that the purpose of this emergency fund account is not to generate interest. I am not investing this money or putting it anywhere that I cannot get to quickly.

It is also important to note that paying off debt should be a higher priority than saving money. Your primary goal is to pay off all debt (except for your mortgage) before you start to save. You cannot save money if you owe money, whether it is credit card debt or student loans.

There are many resources that can provide advice on personal finance. I would recommend professional resources for in-depth financial advice. Dave Ramsey's book, *The Total Money Makeover*[8] has been very helpful for me.

Do make your financial health a priority as it will provide the peace of mind to go after your other life goals.

Steps to take

Use your journal to write down your thoughts on building up some savings.

1. Brainstorm how you can implement the ideas presented in the chapter. Go through all your monthly subscriptions and cancel the ones that you do not need. For example, I found out that I had two subscriptions to an online security tool.

---

[8] Ramsey, Dave. (2009). *The Total Money Makeover: A Proven Plan for Financial Fitness*. Nashville, TN: Thomas Nelson.

2. Wear an outfit over and over again. If it is good enough for Meghan Markle or Kate Middleton, then it is good enough for me. I do not need to buy another outfit for a wedding, gala, or function when I have several in the closet that I have worn before.

3. Sell items in your closet that you do not need. Of course, you could donate them too.

4. Limit dining at restaurants or ordering take out. Admittedly, this is one of the biggest challenges for me because it is hard to find time to cook with a busy schedule. The best way for me to overcome this challenge is to plan out the menu for the week. I prepare two or three of the items on the menu during the weekend and freeze or refrigerate. So, all I have to do during the week is heat up the meals. This is the easiest way to eat well and save time during the week.

5. Start a side hustle. What can you do (time permitting, of course) that could bring in a little extra income?

6. Pay for items with cash. If you cannot pay with cash, then you cannot afford it.

In the final section, we will work on attacking our goals. We will use the information and work we have done in the preceding sections. This next section is our get-to-work section. Are you ready to roll up your sleeves? I am super excited!

Section 6
E is for Execution

Chapter 19
Goal Setting

Ten marathons

I mentioned earlier in the book that my mantra is from **Psalm 18:32**, "It is God who arms me with strength and keeps my way secure."

I am embracing being comfortable with being uncomfortable. I recommend that you seek out hard things to stretch you and expand your horizons.

After I had the twins, I trained for my first marathon to help me shed the baby weight. I ran my first marathon in 2004, and I thought that would be it. At the time, it did not occur to me that I could train for a 5K or a 10K to ease me into running. My pace was a 14:30-minute mile, so I was a very slow runner. For what it is worth, my pace never improved that much beyond a 12-minute mile. So, although I have completed ten full marathons, I still do not consider myself a professional runner.

In 2014, a friend of mine had trained for and run a couple of half marathons. She inspired me to train and run a half marathon. I started to enjoy running, and I liked the mindset that I needed to run a long distance.

In May 2014, I ran my first half marathon race even though I had run a full marathon ten years earlier. I registered for a few more half marathons and continued to train.

I also joined a Nigerian Runners running group I found on Facebook. In the group, every year we would join a challenge to run 1,000 miles for the year. Running became a part of my regular life even though I was still very slow.

One year after I ran my half marathon, I ran my second full marathon. It was brutal, but I was inspired. I made the decision to set a goal of running ten full marathons by May 2020.

In December of 2018, I achieved my goal and ran my tenth (and what was my last) full marathon. Along the way, I also completed fourteen half marathons.

The feeling of setting a tough but realistic goal and achieving it gave me such a confidence boost.

The human mind and body is an amazing thing. If one can set a goal and believe that they can achieve it, and be willing to work hard, anything is possible.

What have you been dreaming about accomplishing that perhaps you think is too hard? How has reading my marathon journey helped you to make a connection to that goal? Does your seemingly impossible goal seem more within reach?

Completing a master's degree with twins

It is important for me to say that completing a master's degree was not originally a goal of mine. Life is full of surprising twists and turns...

I applied to graduate school to study for my master's degree just before I got married. I did not realize that I would become pregnant so quickly after the wedding. I gained admission, and when I realized that I was pregnant, I honestly did not understand what a challenge it would be to complete the program.

It was my first pregnancy, and I did not know what to expect. I decided to start the program, thinking that it would be life as normal. I could have the babies and not miss a beat. Or so I thought.

I started a full-time Master of Business Administration (MBA) program when I was twelve weeks pregnant. And I was exhausted. I did not consider the challenges of such a program while pregnant with twins. I even did the full-time program! No one told me this was a bad idea, so I registered and showed up.

Nothing could have prepared me for how grueling the next two years of my life would be. If I had known it would be that tough, nothing would have convinced me to undertake such a task. Even now I look back and wonder what on earth I was thinking.

At twenty-three weeks, I was put on bed rest because I started to experience contractions. The early mornings for class, the stress of attending classes, and the late night homework left me exhausted.

I had no idea what bed rest meant. I did not understand the severity and could not imagine lying in bed all day.

God was so gracious and full of mercy because I did not adhere to the stay-in-bed rules. I kept attending classes and trying to lighten my schedule.

At thirty-one weeks, I had to suspend school because again, I started to experience contractions. This time there would be no bending the rules. And this time, I did have to stay in bed.

I had to take time off from school until after the twins were born. In total, I was out of school for several months. By the time I returned to school the following fall, my twins were seven months old.

I still do not know how I did it. When I returned to school, I took on an extra course load and was still able to graduate on schedule with my class.

A dear friend of mine (who has since passed from cancer) was staying with us at the time and would watch the twins all day. I would get home from school around 6 p.m. to find her completely exhausted from watching them all day. Remember the babies were still little!

I would bathe the twins, feed them, play with them, and put them to bed. I would then stay up late completing assignments. There would be nights that I would not go to bed at all.

The cycle would begin again the next day.

That was one of the toughest periods of my life. I am not sure I would tell anyone to do anything that aggressive or ambitious.

The message here is two-fold:

1. God provides grace for every situation. He enables us to do what would otherwise be impossible.

2. It is important to maintain momentum. If you or I start something, it is important to keep going and not take a break. It is harder to come back to a tough task after a break than it is to tough it out and complete the task. Attack your goal one milestone at a time. Please remember that you do not need to adopt an all-or-nothing approach. You can set about achieving your goal a little at a time. Don't forget that it's better to work on it for a few minutes each day than to wait for the perfect time to do it all at once.

Visualization

Visualizing yourself as having achieved your goals can be a helpful method to organize your thoughts. Visualization can help you plan out the steps to your destination. Of course, it is not enough to visualize your goals, but beginning with the end in mind is a great way to start.

One way to visualize your end state is through the use of a vision board.

Vision boards became popular as a result of the 2006 best-selling self-help book, *The Secret,* by Rhonda Byrne.

A vision board is a way to focus on the goals that you want to achieve using pictures and images that inspire.

When we talk about visualization, we are speaking about faith—faith that what we desire will be manifested.

Although they can be, vision boards do not have to be based on acquiring material things.

You could start by creating one vision board. This board incorporates the high-level components of the life that you desire.

Or, you could create several vision boards, for each area of your life on which you would like to focus.

At the end of the chapter, we will create a vision board, which is a fun exercise.

Count the cost

Before you start the journey to achieving your goals, it will be important to determine what is involved. If you go into the journey with this knowledge, you will be more likely to stick with it when things get tough. Consider the following:

- What will you have to give up or sacrifice? Is it time spent with friends and loved ones, sleep, TV, or other hobbies?

- How much money will you have to spend to accomplish this goal?

- What will you do when you want to give up? What will you do to keep yourself motivated?

- What skills will you need? What training is required?

- Who will you need to enlist to help pick up the slack? Your spouse? Older children? Even younger children will need to understand that Mummy may not have as much free time.

Let's take a look at the Scripture to understand the cost of pursuing our goals.

> *Large crowds were traveling with Jesus, and turning to them he said: "If anyone comes to me and does not hate father and mother, wife and children, brothers and sisters—yes, even their own life—such a person cannot be my*

disciple. And whoever does not carry their cross and follow me cannot be my disciple.

Suppose one of you wants to build a tower. Won't you first sit down and estimate the cost to see if you have enough money to complete it? For if you lay the foundation and are not able to finish it, everyone who sees it will ridicule you, saying, 'This person began to build and wasn't able to finish.'

Or suppose a king is about to go to war against another king. Won't he first sit down and consider whether he is able with ten thousand men to oppose the one coming against him with twenty thousand? If he is not able, he will send a delegation while the other is still a long way off and will ask for terms of peace. In the same way, those of you who do not give up everything you have cannot be my disciples."

(Luke 14:25–33)

As the Scripture illustrates, before we set about to accomplish a goal (in this case building a tower), it is important to count the cost of what it will take to accomplish this task.

Setting expectations is critical before embarking on a goal, big or small. Don't forget this important step.

S.M.A.R.T. goals

In November 1981, George T. Doran wrote an influential paper. Doran was a consultant and former Director of Corporate Planning for Washington Water Power Company. The paper title was "There's a S.M.A.R.T. Way to Write Management's Goals and Objectives." Since then the S.M.A.R.T. acronym has been used countless times as a goal-setting method.

S.M.A.R.T. stands for

Specific

Measurable

Achievable

Relevant

Time-bound

As you set your goals, it will be beneficial to apply the S.M.A.R.T. method to each goal. This method helps you to break down the goal into something manageable and achievable.

More bang for the buck

I do not want to work harder. I want to work more effectively. I want to get more goals achieved without spending hours on work.

In the world that we live in, often the hardest workers are rewarded with increased responsibilities and more work. Is that really the reward?

I am determined to measure each activity on a scale of aggravation versus reward. If the aggravation is greater than the reward, then to me, that task is not worth doing.

Do not get me wrong, I am an advocate of hard work and of working very hard. Nothing in life comes easy—you have to put in the time to achieve anything.

But, I believe in working smart. Set your goal and put forth the effort. It is helpful to be very clear on your definition of why you're striving for the goal. Every single time, your why will determine whether a goal or an achievement is worth pursuing. Your why is the reward.

I would like you to get honest with yourself here. Spend time delving into each goal that you would like to set for yourself. Is the juice worth the squeeze? Will it be worth it to achieve the goals that you desire? Consider this based on what you learned earlier in the book about self-care. Remember the importance of keeping your engine humming and in good condition.

Steps to take

Use your journal to write about your goals. You can create a vision board later.

Defining your goals

1. Before we make a vision board, let's set some S.M.A.R.T. goals. Here are four categories you could use as inspiration for developing goals:

    a. Financial

    b. Personal

    c. Career/business

d. Overall health and well-being

For each bucket, I would like you to list one short-term goal, one medium-term goal, and one long-term goal. Short-term goals would be achievable within one year. Medium-term goals would be achievable within the next five years. And the long-term goals would be achievable in ten years or more.

2. Now for each goal that you have listed, spend time determining what specific skills and knowledge you will need to achieve each goal. For example, will you need to take an online course? Will you need to return to school? Who do you need to meet with to get knowledge in your interest area?

3. Decide how long you think it will take you to achieve each goal and write down the time you expect to accomplish each goal.

Creating a vision board

Now let's get to work making our vision board to highlight our goals, both short-term and long-term.

What you will need?

1. One poster board per vision board that you plan to make. It should measure at least 24" x 24."

2. Magazines from which you can cut pictures and quotes from. Oprah's magazines are usually a great start. There are so many vision board-friendly pictures to inspire you.

3. A pair of scissors.

4. Glue or sticky tape to stick the pictures to your poster board.

5. Any photos or quotes that you find meaningful. These could include squares with your mantra, a future job title, or photos of family or places you would like to visit.

6. Time! Block out an hour or two to create a vision board that works for you. If you would like to invite a friend or two over to do it as a group, that could be a good bonding activity with your tribe. You may find this to be an exercise that you would like to do on your own. Either way works.

Chapter 20
Time Management

Steven Covey's Four Quadrants

In Steven Covey's book, *The Seven Habits of Highly Effective People*[9], he discusses a habit called, "Putting first things first."

In this habit, he describes four quadrants:

1. Quadrant 1 (Q1) – Urgent and Important

2. Quadrant 2 (Q2) – Not Urgent but Important

3. Quadrant 3 (Q3) – Urgent but Not Important

4. Quadrant 4 (Q4) – Not Urgent and Not Important

---

[9] Covey, Steven R. (1989). *The Seven Habits of Highly effective People* New York, NY: Simon & Schuster.

When I examined these quadrants of my life, I realized that over 50% of my time was being spent in Q1 where everything is an emergency. Of course, if it is an emergency, it has to be important. Sometimes life demands that we operate in this quadrant. But, to avoid stress and burnout, this should not be where we spend most of our time.

In Q3, we operate in a manner that is very like Q1. The difference is that the perceived urgency is based on expectations and pressure from other people. Something may not be important to us, but someone else who is operating in crisis mode may make their emergency ours instead. This tends to happen a lot with interruptions and unplanned phone calls. This could happen at home or at work. It can also happen at work with meetings that suddenly appear on our calendar. Mandatory attendance on short notice can throw off what would otherwise have been a well-planned day.

What is the best way to avoid living life in Q1 and/or Q3? Being able to say no to the things that do not align with our goals and objectives. Be clear on what those goals and objectives are to begin with. That will help us determine whether something is worth our time.

Q4 is pretty obviously our free time or leisure time. I do find myself spending time here, but I'm aware that it's usually to rest or unwind. And usually only for short periods. Mothers have to get a move on!

As F.I.E.R.C.E Mothers, our intent is to live most of our lives in Q2. This is where we find time to plan, set goals, and get to work achieving our goals. It is where we design the life of our dreams. It is often the hardest quadrant in which to live. This is because the activities that fall under this quadrant are not urgent. The typical life of a Mother is run by urgent matters. Mothers always have a full plate, so it is important to identify and prioritize the tasks that will lead to the life of our dreams.

To live a successful life in Q2, we have to become Mothers that focus on the important things. These are things such as:

- spending quality time with each child. My daughter and I plan time to get our nails done together as an example. My older son loves theater, and I do not. But I took him to see a popular show, and that strengthened our bond.

- relaxation time.

- goal setting and working toward the goals.

- our marriage.

- other important relationships.

There will be other important activities for you, of course, and we should prioritize these activities.

We have to apply discipline to focus on those things over less important tasks.

Prioritizing

The following are the top priorities in my life, which come before anything else. These are my Q2 activities around which I have designed my life. There will be times that some of the items in this list fall into the Urgent and Important category, or Q1. This will depend on the day or situation.

1. **A relationship with God**

    - Prayer

    - Bible reading

    - Church

    - Giving

2. **Family**

    - Marriage

    - Children

- Mother

- Siblings

- In-laws

3. **Relationships**

   - Close friends

   - Tribe

4. **Health and fitness**

   - Sleep

   - Exercise

   - Nutrition

5. **Career and work**

   - Job

   - Financial independence

6. **Self-development**

   - Online courses

- Reading

- Training seminars

7. **Hobbies**

- Travel

- Reading for leisure

- Trying new experiences

Steps to take

Write your responses to the following prompts in your journal.

1. List the priorities in your life. These items should be your Q2 focus. If anything does not make it to the list, then it is not important.

2. Schedule time in your day to tackle the items on your priority list. If it does not get scheduled, it does not get done. Please be sure to schedule a time for rest and relaxation.

3. Make a list of activities on which you spend time that do not fall into Q2. How can you start to cut down on the time that you spend on these things? Can you drop these activities altogether?

As we wrap up our journey through this book, I would like to end by providing you with access to more resources. These resources will help you as you design this new F.I.E.R.C.E life.

It is important to identify next steps, so that you can immediately start to work on your goals. It is not enough to just feel good. Being intentional is critical to help you actually make changes because they are changes that will impact your life in a significant fashion.

Chapter 21

Your F.I.E.R.C.E. Future Awaits

It is your time

I wrote this book with you fabulous Mothers at the forefront of my mind. I want to change the way that we Mothers show up in our lives. I want to provide you with the tools to make changes that you thought were impossible before. You can do it! With the right mindset and desire, you are capable of achieving that status of rock star Mother. If you follow the principles in this book, you will become more F.I.E.R.C.E and your life will change.

You can do it. I know that life is challenging for Mothers —we have so many things to juggle. But, I have broken down the principles that I have applied to my own life into smaller segments of the journey. You don't have to face this as an overwhelming mountain to climb. Small steps are key.

It will be a sacrifice to achieve the goals you have set for yourself. You will have to miss a few of your favorite TV shows or cut down on a few social events.

But, please keep the momentum going. Please take action. Do not put this book on the shelf and move on with life as usual. Use it as a reference for continued inspiration or instruction.

I want to hear from you, and I want to hear about some of the changes that you have made to live a F.I.E.R.C.E life. You can reach out to me at ugochi@fiercemothers.com.

Extra materials

I have included exercises in each chapter. These exercises are for you to delve a little deeper and put what you have read into practice.

As you work your way through the book, I have included extra materials. For example, I have included a sample schedule to help you manage your time. There is also a sample budget, which you can download as a starting point and customize as you see fit.

Please visit the website fiercemothers.com/resources to access additional materials.

Next steps

If you would like additional help, I encourage you to check out my website, where I provide information on how to work with me.

Check out the available programs here:
http://fiercemothers.com/more

Regardless of whether or not you want to work with me, I would love to hear about your journey.

You can reach me at ugochi@fiercemothers.com.

Here's to you becoming the next version of yourself. Here's to you F.I.E.R.C.E Mother.

Ugochi Onyewu

About the Author

Ugochi Onyewu is an author, podcaster and ex marathon runner.

Ugochi was born in London and grew up in Nigeria, where she went to High School. She returned to the United Kingdom at age 17, where she attended College and Graduate School. She moved to the United States in March 2000. She lives in the Washington D.C metro area with her husband and three children. This is the first of what Ugochi hopes is many books.

References

Here is a list of creators and authors that I have referenced throughout the book.

1. *Seven Habits of Highly Effective People* by Steven Covey

2. *The Sleep Revolution* by Arianna Huffington

3. *The Miracle Morning* by Hal Elrod

4. *The Total Money Makeover* by Dave Ramsey

5. The "How to Get Rich" Podcast by Naval Ravikant

Bonus Section

The Igbo Initiative Podcast

I host a podcast, which I reference throughout the book, on Igbo culture. The podcast is an open invitation to the world learn more about the culture. Hear from a wide variety of successful women from across the world who are in different walks of life. These women are either of Igbo heritage or friends of Igbo culture. Learn what makes these women successful by listening to their stories.

To access the podcast, visit the website http://www.theigbo.com. You can also listen on Apple Podcasts, Stitcher, Spotify, and Google Play.

A Sampling of Inspiring "The Igbo Initiative" Podcast Guests

It is impossible to pick favorite episodes of The Igbo Initiative Podcast. It's also impossible to include excerpts from every episode of my podcast. Each woman that I have spoken to has left me with something new and inspiring. I love each episode that I have made.

I have curated episodes featuring guests who were there at the beginning of my podcast journey. Each person has a key takeaway, which is important for us to revisit here.

It is important to note that most of these ladies are Mothers. Some women have struggled with impostor syndrome. They have wondered whether their best is ever good enough. They are special but not because of their successes. They are special because each woman refused to give up despite their challenges.

As I read over this chapter, I am inspired all over again. The words on this page renew my determination and motivate me to move forward.

I introduce each guest and provide some background. Then I highlight the key takeaway from each episode.

To listen in more depth, please visit the website at https://www.theigbo.com/podcast.

1. Ayozie Pollendine
Blogger, Artist, and Performer

Ayozie Pollendine is a blogger, artist, and performer. She lives in London with her husband and two daughters.

Ayozie believes that creativity exists in us all, but we just have to find a way to harness that creativity.

Key takeaway

- Journal every day. This process does not have to be complicated. It is as simple as keeping a notebook where you write down specific thoughts.

- Journaling is a great way to help you achieve your goals and promote a sense of well-being. Journaling also has a powerful impact on communication skills, both verbal and written.

- She believes that you should know what you love and be willing to train to be the best that you can be.

2. ChiChi Iro
Founder/CEO of The Enabled Life organization

ChiChi Iro is the founder and CEO of The Enabled Life nonprofit organization. She is the first person with cerebral palsy to graduate from the Nigerian Law School. ChiChi is a Mother to four strapping young men.

The Enabled Life organization is committed to enabling all people living with challenges of any type. The focus is to help individuals with cerebral palsy to live their lives to the fullest.

We discuss forgiveness and the impact her Mother had on her life.

Key takeaway

- Carrying a burden from the past is self-hate. Come to terms with the issues by laying it out on the table. Accept that someone hurt you and try to figure out why the person that hurt you did what they did. But give yourself a reason to forgive them.

3. RiRi Okoye
CEO of Majestically Rare

Rita Okoye, also known as RiRi, is an international events planner and business trainer. Her career has spanned over 20 years. She describes herself as a people person, and serving comes naturally to her. She has worked for the likes of NatWest bank, Financial Times Magazines, Pride Magazine, Channel 5, and the BBC in London. Rita is also a professional speaker. She has spoken for Leap Africa, Lagos Business School, and the University of Lagos to mention a few. In her spare time, she writes a personal development blog at http://www.ririokoye.com.

Riri is also the founder of Raising Confident Girls Initiative. This is a movement with over 26,000 online members on Facebook. The foundation gives back to society by hosting events for Mothers and daughters. The foundation also pays school fees for underprivileged girls.

She is also a Mother of three teenagers, two boys, and a girl.

Key takeaway

- The more you talk about confidence, the more confident you become. You can achieve so much more when you believe in yourself rather than just coasting through life.

- Having self-confidence is a mindset. It is not based on your personality. Instead, it is the ability to believe in your unique gifts and skills.

4. Adanna Onyewuchi
IT Strategy Consultant

Adanna is an infrastructure technology director. She has managed programs that deliver on customers' strategic goals. She is a Mother of three grown children—two young men in their twenties, and a teenage girl.

We talk about what it takes to succeed in the corporate world and beyond regardless of personality.

Key takeaway

- Vocalize your vision for yourself and affirm yourself. Try not to be negative and put yourself down, but speak positively to yourself. Adanna also believes that just like you eat every day, so you should also move every day.

5.Destiny Iheukwumere
Founder of Life Builders Africa Mission

Destiny was born in Uzuakoli, Imo State, Nigeria in 1970. She grew up in Aba.

She knew from a very young age that she was called to help the poor and that she would go into full-time ministry.

Destiny has such a passion for the less fortunate. She often sacrifices her personal needs to help people in distress. She has an amazing story.

She lost her husband and son in the span of a few months. Destiny had to raise two children alone. Both recently graduated from college and are living successful lives.

Today, she is the founder of Life Builders Africa Mission (LBAM). LBAM is a ministry with many arms:

- A school

- Farm

- Widows ministry

- Azalea, a girl to women ministry

- White Oak, a boy to men initiative

- Community care

Additionally, there are plans for LBAM to add a clinic to serve the community.

Key takeaway

God can do amazing things with a life dedicated to Him. No amount of time or resources is too little to make an impact and help to address the huge need in the world.

6.Kwavi Agbeyegbe
Midlife Lifestyle Coach and Midlife Wellness Advocate

Kwavi speaks at various corporations and conferences. She spreads the news of the benefits of living a healthy lifestyle. She has a focus on self-care and mindfulness, both of which have a direct impact on personal and professional well-being. She also helped to put me back on track when I gained fifteen pounds. I mention her earlier in the book.

Kwavi is the Mother of two teenage boys.

In her episode, we discuss thriving in midlife. We also discuss self-care and maintaining a healthy weight.

Key takeaway

Paying attention to your body will make an impact on your health and well-being. Your body will always steer you in the right direction. It is important to listen to the signals it gives you.

7.Chika Ojiaku
Founder of Day MyLane

Chika is the founder and Creative Director of Day MyLane, an apparel company. Chika is another creative who started her journey studying biochemistry. She then went on to law school, and now works in the area of Intellectual Property Protection.

In 2016, Chika started her company Day MyLane. Day MyLane is an apparel line that celebrates cross-cultural universal themes of daily living in a fun and fresh way.

In this episode, we talk about the challenges of starting a new business, how to manage a side hustle while working a full-time job, and maintaining a balanced approach to social media.

Key takeaway

Keep creating great content. You never know who you may impact. You may change a life without getting a "Like" on social media.

8.Adaeze Iheanyi-Igwe
Self-development Explorer, Marathon Runner, and Model

Adaeze is an inspiring lady in midlife. At the young age of forty-four, she decided to go into modeling and is having a fantastic time doing it. She is a Mother of three teenage boys, a Project Manager, and a marathon runner.

In this episode, we discuss her amazing self-development journey.

Key takeaway

If something does not scare you, then it is not big enough. It is never too late to be what you could have been. She translates an old Igbo proverb which says, "Whenever you wake up, that is your morning."

9. Adaeze Enekwechi
Former White House Associate Director for Health Programs

Dr. Enekwechi served as Vice President for Policy, Strategy, and Analytics with McDermott+Consulting. Before, she served as the Associate Director for Health Programs at the White House Office of Management and Budget under President Obama. As the Federal government's chief health care budget official, she provided policy, management, and regulatory oversight for over $1 trillion in spending on a range of federal programs. Those programs include the Centers for Medicare and Medicaid Services, Centers for Disease Control and Prevention, the National Institutes of Health, and all Federal health agencies.

Adaeze is also a Mother of two.

Key takeaway

As you advance, wherever you find yourself, take a seat. If it's at the head of the table, sit comfortably because you will have earned it. Don't let anyone else tell you that you do not belong there. If you are given the responsibility for a task, do way more than is expected. Erase any reasons or excuses not to give you what you deserve.

10. Chioma Onwuanibe
CFO and Personal Finance Guru

Chioma is an accomplished CFO and former investment banker. She graduated with a degree in economics from Princeton University. She then obtained an MBA from the Wharton School at the University of Pennsylvania.

Chioma is the proud Mother of two young men.

Key takeaway

Chioma emphasizes the importance of making connections. Finding something that connects you to the person that you are talking to is important. It is not as important to go to the best schools as it is to be able to articulate what makes you unique.

11.Angela Onwuanibe
Psychiatrist

Dr. Onwuanibe is a board-certified psychiatrist with over thirty years of experience in General Medicine and seventeen years of experience in psychiatry and psychopharmacology. Dr. Onwuanibe provides expert diagnosis and compassionate care for patients with a full range of mental health needs.

In this episode, we discussed various aspects of mental health. We discuss many myths surrounding mental health and specific signs to watch out for in a loved one or oneself.

Angela talks about the importance of paying attention to your mental health and that of your loved ones. She recommends annual mental health checks in the same way we would get annual physicals.

Angela is the Mother of two grown children—a boy and a girl.

Key takeaway

Angela lives by the principles in the book, *The Four Agreements* by Don Miguel Ruiz, and discusses each of the agreements, which are:

1. Be impeccable with your words.

2. Don't take anything personally.

3. Don't make assumptions. Communicate very clearly what your needs are.

4. Do your best. Your best changes at different times.

12. Ada Ibe-Offurum, MD
Founder of Common Ground Network

Ada is an Assistant Professor of Medicine at the University of Maryland School of Medicine.

She is also the founder of the Common Ground Network.

Common Ground is a network of fifty to sixty strong women in the DC, Maryland, and Virginia Area. It was formed in 2005. The network was formed with the premise that everyone needs a community to learn, laugh, share, and make friendships. It was designed to be a natural network for mentorship questions and career guidance in a safe space.

Ada is the proud Mother of three children—two boys, and a girl.

Key takeaway

Take the time to pause and reflect on who you are, what you are good at, and where you would like to go. Identify the areas where you may need help. Make that space for yourself to pause and reflect.

Huge Favor!

Thank you so much for reading my first book!

I appreciate you reading and making it to the back page of my first book. This was a true labor of love, and I would love to hear your thoughts and honest feedback.

Please tell me what you loved. What is your key takeaway?

I would appreciate a helpful review on Amazon.

Thank you so much!
With love,

Ugochi Onyewu

Made in United States
Orlando, FL
09 June 2022

18650343R00145